What Is a Gospel?

What Is a Gospel?

The Genre of the Canonical Gospels

Charles H. Talbert

LONDON

SPCK

First published in the U.S.A. by Fortress Press

First published in Great Britain 1978
SPCK
Holy Trinity Church
Marylebone Road
London NW1 4DU

Printed in Great Britain by Billing & Sons Limited,
Guildford, London and Worcester

ISBN 0 281 03628 4

To
Caroline and Richard

Contents

Abbreviations

BJRL	*Bulletin of the John Rylands Library*
CBQ	*Catholic Biblical Quarterly*
Exp	*Expositor*
ExpT	*Expository Times*
HeyJ	*Heythrop Journal*
HTR	*Harvard Theological Review*
IDB	*The Interpreter's Dictionary of the Bible*
Int	*Interpretation*
JBL	*Journal of Biblical Literature*
JJS	*Journal of Jewish Studies*
JTS	*Journal of Theological Studies*
LCL	Loeb Classical Library
NovT	*Novum Testamentum*
NTS	*New Testament Studies*
RGG	Religion in Geschichte und Gegenwart
SBL	Society of Biblical Literature
TDNT	Theological Dictionary of the New Testament
ZNW	*Zeitschrift für die Neutestamentliche Wissenschaft*
ZTK	*Zeitschrift für Theologie und Kirche*

Foreword

This volume is based upon research that was begun during 1971–72, when my family and I spent a post–doctoral year in Rome under the auspices of the Society for Religion in Higher Education. I owe a debt of gratitude to the Vatican Library and the libraries at the American Academy and the Pontifical Biblical Institute for the rich resources they placed at my disposal.

Grateful acknowledgment is made to The Society of Biblical Literature for permission to use in this book material from my article, "The Concept of Immortals in Mediterranean Antiquity," *Journal of Biblical Literature*, 94 (1975), pp. 419–36. Thanks are also due to the Cambridge University Press for permission to use material from my article, "The Myth of a Descending–Ascending Redeemer in Mediterranean Antiquity," *New Testament Studies*, 22 (1976), pp. 418–439.

The Graduate Council of Wake Forest University has faithfully supported my work on various parts of the project with a series of grants. Without this help my progress would have been hampered.

A number of unnamed friends have read and corrected earlier forms of the manuscript. My debt to them is greater than they realize. The flaws that remain can only be my responsibility.

Most of all, I appreciate the unfailing encouragement of my wife, Betty, and my children, Caroline and Richard.

Wake Forest University
Winston–Salem, North Carolina
Spring 1977

1
The Problem

In literary terms, what are the canonical gospels?[1] Are there among the literary genres of Mediterranean antiquity any to which Matthew, Mark, Luke-Acts, and John belong? This question has received a variety of answers in the past century or so.

Close similarities between these Christian gospels and Graeco-Roman biographies were perceived and inferences drawn from them in the nineteenth and early twentieth centuries. In the last century Ernest Renan (1863) furnishes a good example. He spoke of the gospels as documents which present themselves as biographies of the founder of Christianity. John, he said, was "the biographer of Jesus, as Plato was of Socrates."[2] In Renan's *Life of Jesus* it is assumed that the gospels are biographies. What is at stake is the matter of where among the various types of biographies of antiquity they belong, that is, how reliable they are historically. Renan concludes that the canonical gospels—

> are neither biographies after the manner of Suetonius, nor fictitious legends in the style of Philostratus; they are legendary biographies. I should willingly compare them with the Legends of the Saints, the Lives of Plotinus, Proclus, Isidore, and other writings of the same kind, in which historical truth and the desire to present models of virtue are combined in various degrees.[3]

At the beginning of this century, C. W. Votaw (1915) argued the same basic thesis.[4] Among the biographical writings of the ancient Greek literature, the nearest parallels to the gospels are the books which report the lives of Epictetus, Apollonius, and Socrates. Arrian's *Discourses of Epictetus*, Xenophon's *Memorabilia*, and Philostratus' *Life of Apollonius of Tyana* are "popular biographies" of the same type as the Christian gospels. Votaw and Renan recognized the similarities between the gospels and Graeco-Roman biographies and assumed they belonged to the same genre. The posture of New Testament research since the 1920s, however, has been a different one.

"The canonical gospels are not biographies. They are the apostolic kerygma built up into a vivid narrative form." For over a generation this has been the virtually unchallenged contention of critical scholarship.[5] In the writings of Rudolf Bultmann this contention finds its place in the major synthesis of the last generation's research on Christian origins.[6] The *denial* of significant generic links between the canonical gospels and ancient biographical literature rests upon three foundation pillars: (1) the gospels are mythical, the Graeco-Roman biographies are not; (2) the gospels are cultic, the Graeco-Roman biographies are not; and, (3) while the gospels emerge from a community with a world-negating outlook, the literary biographies are produced by and for a world-affirming people. Each of these pillars needs further examination.

1. Bultmann argued on the one hand that the gospels are different from the Graeco-Roman biographies in that the gospel material is ordered from one dominant point of view, namely, Jesus is the Son of God, the Lord. The unity of these Christian writings is provided by the Christ myth.[7] On the other hand, he contended that the gospels show no interest in Jesus' human personality, his origin, education, or development as a biography would do.[8] In other words, the Christian gospels are mythical, the Graeco-Roman biographies are not.

The roots of this formulation go back to David Friedrich Strauss.[9] According to modern conceptions, so Strauss reasoned, biography treats a *human* subject *developmentally*. In the first place, the hero of a biography must be entirely and clearly human (I,1). In the second place, the career of the human hero must be treated as a pragmatical sequence of events, that is, with reference to their causes and effects (I,4). Given this understanding of biography, Strauss concluded that the "Christ of the church is no subject for biographical narrative" (I,3). Indeed, in the gospels Christ appears "under a form incompatible with biography" (I,4). This is so because he is there the divinely begotten Son or the incarnate Word.[10] The gospels describe Jesus in mythical terms.

Part of this argument of Strauss, Bultmann, and their followers is clearly problematic and derives from a confusion between modern and ancient biography.[11] Modern biography is certainly developmental; ancient biography was not.[12] D. R. Stuart puts it well.

> The ancient biographer was . . . chiefly interested in the man as he was when he had emerged a finished product. The chronicler tended to see in character and personality static things that it was his task to analyze and describe, but with the evolution of which he was only incidentally concerned.[13]

Granting this fact, the essence of the first foundation pillar consists of the contention that whereas biography describes a *human* subject, the gospels speak about Jesus in mythical terms as a *divine* being.

2. Bultmann's second line of argument concerns cult. On the one hand, he says that the Christian gospels grow up from the cult of Christ. They are the cult legends of Christian worship, that is, the community's rationalization of its original ritual. They are distinguished from other cult legends, however, in that their deity is not a purely mythical figure.[14] On the other hand, since they arise from a worshiping community, the gospels do not reveal the individuality of their authors as the Graeco-Roman biographies do.[15]

The roots for this foundation pillar can be traced back to K. L. Schmidt's seminal essay in the Gunkel *Festschrift* (1923).[16] There Schmidt concluded that the Christian gospels were cult legends, that is, they arose out of a worshiping community; they were *Volksbücher* produced by the collective creativity of the *Gemeinde*; and they were *Kleinliteratur* rather than *Hochliteratur*. By contrast, the Graeco-Roman biographies were *Hochliteratur* produced by individual authors for a literary public.

Part of this argument is clearly suspect. On the one hand, as a result of redaction-critical work on the gospels, all of the gospels are today viewed as conscious creations of individual authors, each with his own artistic and theological tendencies and purposes. The gospel writer has become an individual author once again. As

Bornkamm has put it, he is "an individual figure of primitive Christian literary history, even though the hunt for names and biographical traces is renounced."[17]   If one worked with Schmidt's rigid categories, this would classify the gospels as *Hochliteratur*.[18]   On the other hand, ongoing work in Classics has shown that, however valuable the distinction between *Kleinliteratur* and *Hochliteratur* is in general, it is irrelevant in genre discussions.   The *Life of Aesop* and the *Life of Secundus the Silent Philosopher*, published by B. E. Perry, most definitely emerge from popular rather than literary circles, yet they are just as certainly biographies as is Plutarch's *Lives*.[19]   In the light of these two developments, the second foundation pillar is reduced to its essence.   Whereas the Graeco-Roman biographies were written for a public that was not primarily religious, the gospels are cultic, that is, they were produced exclusively for religious purposes.

3. Bultmann's third argument is the claim that the gospels are symbolic of the distinctiveness of the Christian religion as a whole.[20]   Primitive Christianity was eschatological in its self-understanding, that is, it believed that with Christ world history had reached its end.   As a result, these Christians were detached from world history and human culture.   Furthermore, the kerygma was an eschatological message, so response to it involved a detachment from world history and human culture.   The first gospel, Mark, moreover, was a development out of the kerygma.   The literary form *gospel*, therefore, is unique in antiquity.[21]   Whereas the gospels emerge from a community with a world-denying outlook, the Graeco-Roman biographies were produced by and for a world-affirming people.

The roots of this third foundation pillar go back to the thesis of Franz Overbeck (1837–1905), set forth while he served as professor at Basel (1870–1897).[22]   Overbeck's contention was twofold.   On the one side, he argued that there was an absolute contrast between the forms of Christian *Urliteratur* (the New Testament and the Apostolic Fathers) and the patristic writings which used the forms of profane world literature.   On the other side, he believed that the discontinuity in the literary sphere signaled an existential break between primitive Christianity and the later church.   Over-

beck saw in the negating expectation of a near end of the world the
constitutive element of earliest Christianity. When, as a result of
the parousia's delay, the church adjusted to the world, it became an
historical entity and primitive Christianity died. Acceptance of the
forms of the history of profane literature, therefore, was an index of
the noneschatological nature of the accepting church. Conversely,
the absence of the Graeco-Roman literary forms in the early period
was due to the eschatological character of the community. For
Overbeck, then, the uniqueness of the Christian gospels' literary
form was the necessary corollary of his belief in the world-negating
life-style of primitive Christianity. Overbeck's influence on the
critical consensus is pervasive.[23]

In one crucial respect Bultmann differs from Overbeck. Both
work with the assumption that earliest Christianity was eschatological (world-negating). Both believe that at some later point in time
Christianity lost its eschatological world-negating orientation.
Both think that there is a correlation between literary forms employed by the Christians and their stance, whether eschatological
and world-denying or noneschatological and world-affirming. The
difference comes at the identification of the point in time when the
eschatological orientation was lost and the forms of Graeco-Roman
literature began to be used for Christian ends. Overbeck saw the
breaking point somewhere near the middle of the second century,
that is, after the New Testament writings and the Apostolic Fathers.[24] Bultmann, however, saw the loss of eschatological
consciousness occurring already within the New Testament.
Whereas Mark is a development of the kerygma and, therefore, a
distinctive Christian literary type, reflecting the eschatological
orientation of primitive Christianity, 'the author of Luke-Acts
"endeavors *as a historian* to describe the life of Jesus in his Gospel"
(italics mine) and to write a *history* of the early church in Acts,
reflecting his loss of an eschatological sense.[25] Within the canon
Mark is a gospel, a uniquely Christian literary form, arising out of
the eschatological world-negating kerygma; Luke-Acts, however, is
the first life of Jesus followed by the first history of the church,
written because of its author's loss of an eschatological orientation.
For the third Evangelist, Jesus is the beginning of the history of

Christianity.[26] If Bultmann had accepted Overbeck's dictum that patristic literature begins where one finds Christian use of the forms of Graeco-Roman literature,[27] then he would have found the roots of patristics already in the New Testament, for example, in Luke-Acts.

This distinction in Bultmann between Mark as *gospel* and Luke-Acts as *history* or *biography* is highly problematic.[28] If two so similar writings as Mark and Luke do not belong to the same genre, then genre distinctions seem devoid of any meaning. Even so, one still has to face the third foundation pillar in its Overbeckian simplicity. The distinctive eschatological self-understanding or life orientation of earliest Christianity demanded distinctive literary forms for its expression. Taken together, these three foundation pillars support the battle cry of the critical consensus: "The gospels in the New Testament are not biographies."

Implicit in these three arguments are the criteria assumed, by Bultmann and others in the critical consensus, to be necessary for establishing the genre of a document. Pillar one says that the organizing principle of the whole is crucial. Myth gives the canonical gospels their outer form or *structure*, because it is that which supplies the framework for the material about Jesus' life. If it is conceded that the gospels belong to an ancient literary genre, it must be one in which the structure is supplied by myth. Pillar two implies that purpose or *function* is essential to genre identifications. Since the gospels function within a religious community (cultic context), any genre into which they are claimed to fit must have a cultic purpose. Pillar three assumes that *attitude* or mood is decisive for genre decisions. The gospels, supposedly world-denying in attitude, cannot belong to any genre with a different mood. From these arguments as used by Bultmann in denying the canonical gospels' participation in the ancient biographical genre, one would infer that he believed genre identifications were possible only where there was a conjunction of structure, function, and attitude.

This Bultmannian stance is not far from the views of modern critics. René Wellek and Austin Warren, for example, claim that "genre should be conceived . . . as a grouping of literary works based . . . upon both outer form (specific meter or *structure*) and also upon inner form (*attitude*, tone, *purpose* . . .)" (italics mine).[29] Bultmann's point about myth appears to be the equivalent of Wellek's and Warren's about outer form or structure; his points about function and attitude seem similar to theirs about inner form (attitude and purpose). There is, then, no real complaint to be made about his implied criteria, only about their application.

The critical consensus *affirms* that the literary form *gospel* developed out of the kerygma. The germ cell, Bultmann says, was the kerygma of the death and resurrection of Jesus. It was expanded in a number of stages: (a) the account of the Baptist and the proofs of fulfilled prediction were included to give fuller visualization to the kerygma of the passion and Easter and to assign it a place in the divine plan of salvation; (b) other material was included because the Christian sacraments had to be accounted for in the life of Jesus, the cultically worshiped Lord; (c) miracle stories were incorporated into "the gospel" since Jesus' life, considered divine, served as proof of his authority; (d) apophthegms came into the collection also as visualizations of Jesus' authority. They in turn occasioned the inclusion of other sayings; (e) the sayings of Jesus were included because, for Christian congregations, Jesus in his role of teacher was important; (f) current exhortations and congregational regulations currently in force were taken into "the gospel" because such regulations had to be accounted for in the life and words of Jesus.[30] This means that, as a literary form, the gospel is a collection of materials used to expand the kerygma. For Bultmann and others of the critical consensus, the gospel is merely the end product of a traditio-historical development or evolution that is unrelated to the generic forms which existed independently of the milieu in which the Jesus tradition moved.[31]

To sum up: the critical consensus works with an assumption that the literary genre of the canonical gospels is defined by their *content*. The gospel is an expansion of the cross-resurrection kerygma. This kerygma is the distinctively Christian message, and the gospel, therefore, is a unique literary form. Comparisons in terms of structure, function, and attitude, moreover, exclude the gospel's belonging to any other ancient genre.

Today there is widespread dissatisfaction with the critical consensus on its view of the genre *gospel*. This dissatisfaction has at least three roots.

In the first place, a changed theological climate has made possible and even encouraged a challenge to the accepted view. R. P. Martin has noted that—

> in the history of interpretation, the search for contemporary parallels to the literary type (or *Gattung*) of 'Gospel' in the popular literature of the ancient world was not likely to seem very fruitful in the 1920s when the uniqueness of the Christian message was receiving emphasis from Karl Barth's stress on the gospel's transcendental qualities as the unrivaled Word of God.[32]

Whereas Neo-Orthodoxy, in its reaction to Liberal Theology, emphasized the discontinuity between early Christianity and culture, the theological mood since the mid-sixties has fostered a reaffirmation of the continuities between religion and culture. In New Testament studies this has found expression not only in the dialogue between biblical critics and modern literary critics generally, but also in the renewed interest in the links between primitive Christianity and its non-Christian environment. This quest has a broad focus, including not only a concern for parallel religious ideas and practices but also parallel literary forms and rhetorical devices. In this kind of theological environment, the claim that the gospels emerged *sui generis* from the uniqueness of Christianity is automatically suspect. Given this theological change, it is no surprise to hear the question, "What is a gospel?" raised again. Nor is it surprising to find challenged the claim of the critical consensus that the canonical gospels are a uniquely Christian genre.

In the second place, certain questions raised by ongoing work on Christian origins have pointed toward the need to reconsider the matter of the genre of the gospels. At least three specific areas merit attention:

1. *The Apocryphal Gospels.* Starting from a study of the apocryphal gospels, Helmut Koester has argued[33] that their forms

are not developments from those of the canonical gospels but are rather related to earlier types of gospel literature such as sayings collections, aretalogies (miracle collections), and apocalypses. As a result, the *Coptic Gospel of Thomas* should be seen in a trajectory from Q, the *Infancy Gospel of Thomas* from collections like the Johannine *Semeia* source, and the *Apocryphon of John* from revelations like the Apocalypse of John. There were, then, four types of primitive Christian gospels: sayings gospels, miracle gospels, revelation gospels, and the canonical type of gospel. The first three types have parallels in the non-Christian world: sayings gospels in the *logoi sophou*, miracle gospels in the Hellenistic collections of miracles, and revelation gospels in Jewish apocalypses. The fourth type, however, the canonical gospel, was created by the creed of Jesus' death and resurrection. This type included within itself, nevertheless, materials from the other three, digesting each different type and making it subservient to its own point of view.

Koester's study assumes that "gospel" applies to the various collections of Jesus material which have a specific christological orientation—of whatever kind—and which seek to mediate faith, however understood. It holds that three of the four types of gospels have analogues in the non-Christian world. Although Koester stops short of claiming a parallel for the canonical gospel type and reverts to the Bultmannian assertion that the four canonical gospels were produced by the kerygma, the impetus of his work nevertheless raises the fundamental question: Is there an analogue for the canonical gospels in the non-Christian world? Later work by Koester indicates his hunch. The canonical gospels are aretalogical biographies, biographies of an "individual whose deeds, words, and death are authorized by the demonstration of divine power and divine presence."[34]

2. *The Gospel of John.* The heritage of the last generation's research, as enshrined in the commentaries on the Fourth Gospel by C. H. Dodd and Rudolf Bultmann, has supplied us with the working hypothesis that John and the Synoptics are independent of one another. James M. Robinson has seen that this hypothesis poses the problem of explaining how the same Gattung could emerge

independently in two different trajectories, the synoptic and the Johannine.[35] If, as is usually supposed, Mark was the creator of the literary genre *gospel* and if John was independent of Mark, where did the fourth Evangelist get his pattern?

Robinson's solution is to attribute the emergence of this new Gattung to a certain configuration in the development of primitive Christianity which made it possible for two authors, independently of each other, at the same stage in the development to do the same thing.[36] Matthew and Luke independently merge Mark and Q, and analogously we may view Mark and John as independently merging a miracle tradition and a passion narrative.[37] If both the second and the fourth Evangelists wanted to correct a misuse of the miracle tradition by use of the passion kerygma, then we can explain how the two, independently of each other, represent the shift from an aretalogy (miracle) type of gospel to the canonical-creedal type. At the same time that he proposes this way of dealing with the problem, Robinson hints at more. "Of course the newness—not to say uniqueness—of the Gattung may well have been exaggerated by dialectic theology," he says in one place.[38] In another, he states that "the view that one distinctive Gattung Gospel emerged *sui generis* from the uniqueness of Christianity seems hardly tenable."[39] The emergence of Mark and John independently points to the necessity for a reexamination of the question of the genre of the canonical gospels.

3. *The Gospel of Mark.* Redaction criticism has derived the theology of Matthew and Luke primarily from the observation of the consistently tendentious ways in which the Evangelists edit a written source available to us for control (Mark). This method has not been as fruitful in the case of Mark as in the case of Matthew and Luke, however, chiefly because of the absence of surviving written sources used by Mark. The oral sources which can be reconstructed behind the Second Gospel are conjectural and there is a probability that a redactor would be inclined to recast oral traditions more freely than a written source. The result is that in this age of redaction criticism, "the absence of surviving written sources of Mark has tended to leave Mark in obscurity."[40]

Given this fact, James Robinson has proposed a shift from deriving an Evangelist's theology from observation of how he edits a known written source (redaction criticism) to "observation of the way he assembles discernible building blocks into a meaningful structure whose form reflects his tendency or theology (*Gattungsgeschichte*)."[41] In so doing, Robinson's struggle to discern the theology of Mark has pointed towards the question of the genre of the canonical gospels.

In the third place, the revival of interest in literary genres after a period of eclipse[42] has occurred at just the moment when New Testament scholars are theologically open and methodologically ready for genre criticism.[43] In the last decade, critics have seen that a particular text standing alone poses a problem because it lacks meaning. The interpretative rule, "What is said must be understood in its context," works well for a word in a sentence, for a sentence in a paragraph, for a paragraph in a section, and for a section in the document as a whole. But what is the context for the whole? This question has led criticism to attempt to view the individual text (i.e., the document as a whole) in terms of a universal type or genre which is constructed on the basis of an inductive grouping of texts with common features. It is the particular text's participation in the universal type or genre that gives it a first level of meaning. "All understanding of verbal meaning is necessarily genre-bound."[44] The particular text's transformation of the genre is then seen as a further way of saying something about the meaning of the document as a whole. An author communicates not only through a system of shared conventions (a genre), but also through modifications of those conventions.[45] Such a literary perspective renders problematic any interpreter's claim that a given document is literarily unique. The ability of the interpreter to find meaning in a writing depends on his being able to see it as part of a larger group of texts. A totally novel form would be unintelligible.[46] A New Testament scholar who is sensitive to the trends in the larger world of literary criticism cannot help but ask the question: "Into what larger context do the canonical gospels fit?"[47]

Several alternatives have been proposed to the thesis that the canonical gospels are developments out of the kerygma and are, therefore, a unique literary type. One group of proposals looks to the *Graeco-Roman milieu* for the clue to the genre of the canonical gospels.[48] Two major attempts may be mentioned. First, Moses Hadas and Morton Smith have argued that the gospels belong to a certain species of biography, aretalogy.[49] An aretalogy, as Hadas defines it, is—

> a formal account of the remarkable career of an impressive teacher that was used as a basis for moral instruction. The preternatural gifts of the teacher often included the power to work wonders; often his teaching brought him the hostility of a tyrant, whom he confronted with courage and at whose hands he suffered martyrdom. Often the circumstances of his birth or his death involve elements of the miraculous.[50]

In a later article, Smith has narrowed the circle. An aretalogy has no precise formal definition but is determined by its content. "It must have a hero whom it celebrates by reporting one or more of his marvelous deeds."[51] Smith's position is summarized in two contentions: (1) many accounts of ancient "divine men" are variants of a recognizable aretalogical form; (2) the gospels are more similar to these accounts than to any other ancient non-Christian works we know. This definition of an aretalogy as a collection of miracle stories is the one most usually accepted today.[52] Also, generally acknowledged is the fact that some evidence points to such collections being sometimes connected with temples of various deities.[53]

The Hadas-Smith thesis has provoked considerable discussion but little support. Its most obvious problem is that, "we have no complete text surviving from the past specifically labeled aretalogy."[54] Given this fact, to attempt to clarify the meaning of the gospels by grouping them with a type of writing with no known surviving examples is to try to understand the known by an appeal to the unknown. At best, this is a dubious procedure. Another problem with the thesis has surfaced in the criticism of Howard Clark Kee who has collected evidence which shows that there is no guarantee that the appearance in two different literatures of antiquity of a rhetorical form, even with similar content, would fulfill the same function in both cases.[55] This has the effect of arguing that genre cannot be determined by content alone, as Smith desires, but only by a conjunction of content, form, and function. For Kee, the *function* of a document is the essential clue to its genre classification.[56] Using such a criterion, Kee regards the gospels as uniquely Christian. To sum up: the Hadas-Smith thesis has failed to convince most scholars.

A second attempt to locate the clue to the genre of the gospels in the Graeco-Roman milieu is that of Philip Shuler who has proposed that the synoptic gospels belong to Mediterranean antiquity's genre of laudatory or encomium biography.[57] This genre, represented by Xenophon's *Agesilaus*, Isocrates' *Evagoras*, Philo's *Life of Moses*, Tacitus' *Agricola*, and Lucian's *Life of Demonax*, had as its primary concern the greatness and merit of individuals. Its purpose was to build a case for the praise of its subject. This *bios* genre existed prior to the Christian gospels and was widely known so that it was available for appropriation by the Evangelists.

This position has the merit of dealing with a genre known from existing examples and from rhetorical reflection about it. It is also argued with a thoroughness that is necessary if the critical consensus is to be overthrown; it stands as the best effort to date on behalf of the biographical position. At the same time, two reservations must be voiced. First, Shuler has used statements in Polybius (*Histories* 10:21 [24]), Cicero (*Epistulae ad Familiares* 5:12), Cornelius Nepos ("Pelopidas" 16:1:1), Plutarch ("Alexander" 1), and Lucian (*How To Write History*, 7) to establish the ancients' consciousness of laudatory biography. There is a discrepancy here. At least some of the references are to biography generally (at least Nepos and Plutarch). Most of them would cover not only encomium but also the peripatetic and popular types. Only the Alexandrian biographies would be excluded.[58] So, while antiquity definitely knew encomium biographies of the nature Shuler describes, the references cited can not be restricted in their intention to that type alone; more precision is needed. Second, the serious weakness of this thesis is its failure to come to terms with the criteria employed by the critical consensus as seen in Bultmann. Hence, Shuler says nothing of biographical structure determined by myth or of the cultic function of Graeco-Roman biographies. No attempt is made to come to terms with the claim that the world-denying attitude of the gospels excludes their participation in the encomium type biography. Shuler's is a good start, but not the final word.

Another group of proposals looks to the *Jewish milieu* for the clue to the genre of the canonical gospels. Although the suggestions that the canonical gospels are to be understood in light of Old Testament models such as the Elisha stories[59] or the Moses legends[60] have been in the nature of hints, M. D. Goulder has recently proposed a full-scale midrashic hypothesis.[61] By *midrash* he means a new interpretation of a sacred text in the light of fresh insight and new experience.[62] Jewish midrash, he says, has four subtypes: (1) versions, like the LXX and the targums; (2) rewritings, like Chronicles and Jubilees; (3) juristic commentaries, like the *Mekilta* and *Sifre*; and, (4) homiletic matter, like *Midrash Rabbah*.[63] Goulder proposes that Matthew is a midrashic expansion of Mark in the manner of the second of these subtypes.[64] Further, the *Sitz im Leben* for Matthew's midrashic activity is the church's celebration of the Jewish festal year. The gospel was written to be read in church around the year.[65] If Matthew is taken as the norm, a gospel is not a literary genre at all but rather a liturgical genre. It is a lectionary book, a series of "Gospels" used in public worship week by week.[66] Luke, according to Goulder, is a midrash on Matthew.[67] Luke also provides readings for a Christian year, but follows the sabbath cycle and not the festal cycle.[68] Mark is also a book of "Gospels" for half a year, that is, from the Jewish New Year on the first of Tishri to Easter. Mark's incompleteness was the invitation for Matthew to embroider the earlier account.[69]

In Goulder's scheme the basic component is the view that each of our synoptic gospels was written to serve as lectionary material for a Christian church, parallel with the Jewish system of readings used by that congregation. Mark was a midrash on the Old Testament readings, as in subtype 4; Matthew was a midrash on Mark, as in subtype 2; and, Luke was a midrash on Matthew, also as in subtype 2. Hence, the canonical gospels—at least the Synoptics —belong to the Jewish genre midrash. As such they could fit into a history of Jewish literature but not into Graeco-Roman literary history.

Goulder's book is learned and provocative. To come out where he does, however, requires one to believe too many improbable things before breakfast.[70] For example, to agree with him we must grant that, (1) the practice of writing a book specifically for lectionary purposes is as old as the Chronicler (but Goulder's case is not made here); (2) the divisions of Codex Alexandrinus do not merely have liturgical significance but were original (which is by no means probable); (3) there exist demonstrable allusions in the appropriate pericopae of Matthew (also Mark and Luke) to the alleged *sidrah* of the day (a case Goulder can sometimes make and sometimes not); (4) all of the material in Matthew not taken over from Mark is created by Matthew, including most of the Sermon on the Mount and most of the parables (which one is reluctant to concede); (5) Matthew is significantly influenced by Paul's theology (a thing not easy to see); and, (6) Mark and Luke, as well as Matthew, reflect a significant allegiance to synagogue practices (which is not at all easy to grant). In the end, one must conclude that Goulder has not made his case. There remains considerable discontent with the critical consensus, but there exists at this time no viable alternative.

This volume shares the current dissatisfaction with the critical consensus that the canonical gospels are not biographies but are *sui generis*. Its purpose is to show that the canonical gospels do, in fact, belong to antiquity's genre of biography. It will accept Bultmann's assumed criteria for determining genre: there must be agreement in a conjunction of outer form (mythical structure), function (cultic), and attitude, if the canonical gospels are to be grouped with any known genre(s) in Mediterranean antiquity.

The plan of our work will unfold accordingly. First, the question will be raised whether or not the canonical gospels and any of the Graeco-Roman biographies shared a common outer form or structure determined by myth. This will be undertaken in Chapters 2 and 3. In these two chapters we will attempt to show that myth supplies the structure not only for the canonical gospels but also for certain ancient biographies. Indeed, the Synoptics will be shown to be shaped by exactly the same myth as some of the biographies, whereas the Fourth Gospel stands alone in using a myth not employed by ancient biographers. Second, the matter of function must be dealt with in detail. Did any of the Graeco-Roman biographies function cultically as the canonical gospels did? In Chapter 4 we will show that some did. Third, the issue of attitude will be taken up. We will ask whether or not the mood of the Christians reflected in the canonical gospels would have been so different from that of the biographies as to preclude any points of contact. We will show that the Christians' outlook in no way excluded self-expression in the literary genres of their milieu. The aim of this volume is to show that there is an agreement between the canonical gospels and certain Graeco-Roman biographies in a conjunction of mythical structure, cultic function, and an attitude of world involvement. When this has been done, our conclusion can be drawn: the canonical gospels belong to the biographical genre of antiquity.

EXCURSUS: BIOGRAPHY

It would be well at this point to say what we mean by biography. This may be done through a comparison of biography, history, and romance in antiquity. Our comparison of biography and history must treat contents, form, and function. In its contents history usually tends to focus on the distinguished and significant acts of great men in the political and social spheres. Biography is concerned with the study of character or the essence of the individual. This difference can be seen most clearly where history most nearly approaches biography, in the historical monograph (e.g., Sallust's *Catiline* and *Jugurtha*) which concentrates primarily upon one individual. Nevertheless, the historical monograph is not biography. The two examples cited are not biographies. They do not attempt to set forth the particularity of the individual's life, i.e., to show first and foremost his individual essence. They aim to narrate political events with which individuals were associated. In antiquity, history was concerned with a man's place in the process of political and social events. Biography was interested in the individual's character, his involvement in a historical process being important only insofar as it reveals his essence.

In form and function history and biography are also different. In *form*, though both are prose narration, history attempts to give a detailed account in terms of causes and effects of events, whereas biography presents a highly selective, often anecdotal, account of an individual's life with events chosen to illumine his character. The comparison of *function* is made difficult by the different kinds of history and biography. At least two different types of historical writing must be mentioned. Political history such as Polybius wrote was intended to provide useful training and experience for the practical politician. Rhetorical history such as we find in Dionysius of Halicarnassus was designed primarily to give pleasure to citizens. Similarly, two different tendencies in biography should be noted. The encomium (e.g., Isocrates, *Evagoras*) and peripatetic type of biography (e.g., Plutarch, *Parallel Lives*) both were intended to provide patterns for imitation. Hence their purpose was moral and ethical, i.e., to build character. The Alexandrian type of biography (e.g., Suetonius, *Lives of the Caesars*) was primarily informative with no special moral objective.

Comparing romance with the other two ancient genres yields what results? The contents of a romance are fictitious, focusing on the experience and emotions of private individuals devoid of historical reality. Both history and biography, however legendary, claim to speak of actual people and events: the former of things that really happened in the corporate affairs of men, the latter of historical facts which reveal the essence of some individual. The form of all three genres is the basic structural pattern of narration. In function, romance aims at nothing more than outright entertainment. There is no desire to inform. History and biography, however, both seek to impart information, the one about corporate matters so as either to instruct statesmen or to entertain citizens, the other to convey the particularity of an individual either as an end in itself or for an ethical objective.

To summarize: ancient biography is prose narration about a person's life, presenting supposedly historical facts which are selected to reveal the character or essence of the individual, often with the purpose of affecting the behavior of the reader.

NOTES

1. Though the question of the literary genre of the apocryphal gospels is also important, this study limits itself to the canonical four.

2. Ernest Renan, *The Life of Jesus* (Garden City, N.Y.: Doubleday & Co., n.d.), p. 136.

3. *Ibid.*, p. 33.

4. Originally published in the *American Journal of Theology* (1915); reprinted as *The Gospels and Contemporary Biographies in the Greco-Roman World* (Philadelphia: Fortress, 1970), with an introduction by John Reumann.

5. Without attempting to be exhaustive, we may mention the following: Franz Overbeck (cf. notes 22 and 24); Paul Wendland, *Die hellenistisch-Römische Kultur: Die Urchristlichen Literaturformen*, 2nd & 3rd eds. (Tübingen: J.C.B. Mohr Paul Siebeck, 1912), p. 273; Karl Ludwig Schmidt (cf. n. 26); Rudolf Bultmann (cf. n. 6); Joachim Jeremias, *The Problem of the Historical Jesus* (Philadelphia: Fortress, 1964), p. 13; C. H. Dodd, *The Apostolic Preaching* (New York: Harper, 1935), p. 47; F. C. Grant, *The Gospels: Their Origin and Growth* (New York: Harper & Brothers, 1957), p. 37; E. Dinkler, *Peake's Commentary on the Bible*, M. Black and H. H. Rowley, eds. (London: Thomas Nelson and Sons, 1962), p. 683; Eduard Schweizer, *The Good News according to Mark* (Richmond: John Knox, 1970), p. 23; Norman Perrin, "The Literary *Gattung* 'Gospel'—Some Observations," *Expository Times*, 82 (1970), 4–7; C. F. Evans, *The Cambridge History of the Bible*, P. R. Ackroyd and C. F. Evans, eds. (Cambridge: Cambridge University Press, 1970), Vol. 1, p. 270; Barnabas Lindars, *The Gospel of John* (London: Oliphants, 1972), p. 25; R. H. Gundry, "Recent Investigations into the Literary Genre 'Gospel'," *New Dimensions in New Testament Study*, R. N. Longenecker, and M. C. Tenney, eds. (Grand Rapids: Zondervan, 1974), pp. 97–114; Beda Rigaux, *The Testimony of St. Mark* (Chicago: Franciscan Herald Press, 1966), p. 6, is more cautious when he says Mark is not a biography "in the modern sense of the word."

6. Rudolf Bultmann, "Evangelien," in *Die Religion in Geschichte und Gegenwart*, H. Gunkel *et al*, eds., 2nd ed. (Tübingen: J. C. B. Mohr Paul Siebeck, 1928), Vol. 2, cols. 418–422, ET in J. Pelikan, ed., *Twentieth Century Theology in the Making* (New York: Harper & Row, 1971), Vol. 1, pp. 86–92; *The History of the Synoptic Tradition* (New York: Harper & Row, 1963), pp. 373–74; *Theology of the New Testament* (New York: Scribner's, 1951), Vol. 1, p. 86.

7. Rudolf Bultmann, *Twentieth Century Theology*, Vol. 1, pp. 88–89. Cf. Julius Schniewind, *Euangelion: Ursprung und Erst Gestalt des Begriffs Evangelium* (Gütersloh, 1927; reprinted, Darmstadt: Wissenschaftliche Buchgesellschaft, 1970), p. 373.

8. Rudolf Bultmann, *Twentieth Century Theology*, Vol. 1, p. 87.

9. David F. Strauss, *A New Life of Jesus*, 2nd ed. (London: Williams & Norgate, 1879), Vol. 1.

10. Cf. Martin Kähler, *The So-Called Historical Jesus and the Historic, Biblical Christ* (Philadelphia: Fortress, 1964), pp. 53–54.

11. D. A. Russell, *Plutarch* (London: Duckworth, 1973), p. 101, points out that *bion graphein* carries connotations alien to modern concepts of biography.

12. *Ibid.*, pp. 102, 115; Arnaldo Momigliano, *The Development of Greek Biography* (Cambridge, Mass.: Harvard University Press, 1971), p. 13; G. N. Stanton, *Jesus of Nazareth in New Testament Preaching* (Cambridge: Cambridge University Press, 1974), p. 121.

13. D. R. Stuart, *Epochs of Greek and Roman Biography* (Berkeley: University of California Press, 1928), p. 178.

14. Rudolf Bultmann, *Twentieth Century Theology*, Vol. 1, pp. 88–89. Cf. Edgar Hennecke, *New Testament Apocrypha*, W. Schneemelcher, ed. (Philadelphia: Westminster, 1963), Vol. 1, p. 80.

15. *Ibid.*, p. 87.

16. Karl Ludwig Schmidt, "Die Stellung der Evangelien in der allgemeinen Literaturgeschichte," in *Eucharisterion. Herman Gunkel zum 60. Geburtstag*, H. Schmidt, ed. (Göttingen: Vandenhoeck & Ruprecht, 1923), pp. 50–134, especially pp. 76, 124.

17. Cited by R. P. Martin, *New Testament Foundations: Volume 1, The Four Gospels* (Grand Rapids: Eerdmans, 1975), p. 234.

18. G. N. Stanton, *Jesus of Nazareth in New Testament Preaching*, p. 125.

19. B. E. Perry, ed., *Aesopica: A Series of Texts Relating to Aesop, Volume 1: Greek and Latin Texts* (Urbana: University of Illinois Press, 1952); *Secundus the Silent Philosopher* (American Philosophical Association, 1964).

20. Rudolf Bultmann, *Twentieth Century Theology*, Vol. 1, p. 89.

21. Rudolf Bultmann, *Theology of the New Testament*, Vol. 1, p. 86.

22. Franz Overbeck, "Über die Anfänge der patristischen Literatur," *Historische Zeitschrift*, n.f. 12 (1882), 417–72. Cf. Philip Vielhauer, "Overbeck, Franz Camille," *Die Religion in Geschichte und Gegenwart*, 3rd ed. (Tübingen: J. C. B. Mohr Paul Siebeck, 1960), Vol. 4, cols. 1750–52.

23. E.g., Amos Wilder, *The Language of the Gospel* (New York: Harper & Row, 1964), p. 44; Eckhard Plümacher, *Lukas als hellenisti-*

scher Schriftsteller (Göttingen: Vandenhoeck & Ruprecht, 1972), Chap. 1; William G. Doty, *Contemporary New Testament Interpretation* (Englewood Cliffs: Prentice-Hall, 1972), p. 132.

24. Franz Overbeck, "Über die Anfänge der patristischen Literatur," pp. 443–44. In this article of 1882, Overbeck was already claiming that the form "gospel" was an original *Gattung* with which Christianity enriched literature (p. 443).

25. Rudolf Bultmann, *Theology of the New Testament*, Vol. 2, p. 117. Cf. Günther Bornkamm, *Paul* (New York: Harper & Row, 1971), pp. xv–xvii, and F. F. Bruce, "The New Testament and Classical Studies," *NTS*, 22 (1976), 235, for a similar point of view.

26. Rudolf Bultmann, *Theology of the New Testament*, Vol. 2, p. 117. Cf. Ernst Käsemann, "The Problem of the Historical Jesus," in *Essays on New Testament Themes* (London: SCM, 1964), pp. 28–29.

27. Franz Overbeck, "Über die Anfänge der patristischen Literatur," p. 444.

28. Rudolf Bultmann, *Theology of the New Testament*, Vol. 1, p. 86. So also are recent attempts to speak of Mark and John as gospels but of Matthew as a church manual and Luke–Acts as history (Cf. Norman Petersen, "So-called Gnostic Type Gospels and the Question of the Genre 'Gospel'," working paper for Task Force on the Gospel Genre, Society of Biblical Literature, 1970, pp. 26–29).

29. René Wellek and Austin Warren, *Theory of Literature*, 3rd ed. (New York: Harcourt, Brace & World, 1956), p. 231. Roger D. Abrahams, "The Complex Relations of Simple Forms," in *Folklore Genres*, Dan Ben-Amos, ed. (Austin: University of Texas Press, 1976), p. 196, says: "We name most traditional genres through a combination of patterns of form, content, and context." Dan Ben-Amos, *Ibid.*, p. 225, says each genre is characterized by a set of relations between form, theme, and social usage.

30. Rudolf Bultmann, *Theology of the New Testament*, Vol. 1, p. 86.

31. Norman Petersen, "So-called Gnostic Type Gospels and the Question of the Genre 'Gospel'," pp. 40, 45, 53.

32. R. P. Martin, *New Testament Foundations*, Vol. 1, p. 19. James M. Robinson has made much the same point in *Jesus and Man's Hope* (Pittsburgh: Pittsburgh Theological Seminary, 1970), Vol. 1, p. 104.

33. Helmut Koester, "One Jesus and Four Primitive Gospels," in James M. Robinson and Helmut Koester, *Trajectories through Early Christianity* (Philadelphia: Fortress, 1971), pp. 158–204.

34. Helmut Koester, "Romance, Biography, and Gospel," working paper for the Task Force on the Genre of the Gospels, Society of Biblical Literature, 1972, p. 147 of the collection; p. 27 of the individual paper.

35. James M. Robinson, "On the *Gattung* of Mark (and John)," in *Jesus and Man's Hope*, Vol. 1, p. 104; and "The Johannine Trajectory," in *Trajectories through Early Christianity* (Philadelphia: Fortress, 1971), p. 266. This problem was recognized earlier by Otto A Piper, "The Origin of the Gospel Pattern," *JBL*, 78 (1959), 115–124. Piper conveniently assembled various answers to the question but made no advance beyond the critical consensus.

36. James M. Robinson, *Trajectories through Early Christianity*, pp. 234–35.

37. James M. Robinson, "The Problem of History in Mark Reconsidered," *Union Seminary Quarterly Review*, 20 (1965), 136–37. This, of course, runs counter to the claim that John's *Semeia* source included a passion narrative. Cf. Robert T. Fortna, *The Gospel of Signs* (Cambridge: Cambridge University Press, 1970).

38. James M. Robinson, *Trajectories*, p. 268.

39. *Ibid.*, p. 235. In *A New Quest of the Historical Jesus* (Naperville: Alec R. Allenson, 1959), p. 55, Robinson still followed the critical consensus.

40. James M. Robinson, *Jesus and Man's Hope*, Vol. 1, p. 104.

41. *Ibid.*, Vol. 1, p. 102.

42. Eliseo Vivas, "Literary Classes: Some Problems," *Genre*, I (1968), 97–105.

43. E.g., William G. Doty, "The Concept of Genre in Literary Analysis," working paper for the Task Force on the Genre of the Gospels, Society of Biblical Literature, 1972, pp. 29–64 of the collection. This paper was produced after its author had spent a post-doctoral year (1971–72) working on nontheological literary criticism. *SBL Seminar Papers, 1972*, Vol. 2, pp. 413–48.

44. E. D. Hirsch, Jr., *Validity in Interpretation* (New Haven: Yale University Press, 1967), p. 76.

45. Alastair Fowler, "The Life and Death of Literary Forms," in *New Directions in Literary History*, Ralph Cohen, ed. (Baltimore: Johns Hopkins University Press, 1974), p. 77.

46. René Wellek and Austin Warren, *Theory of Literature*, p. 245.

47. Norman Petersen, "So-called Gnostic Type Gospels and the Question of the Genre 'Gospel'," p. 19, says: "From the perspective of

genre criticism, redaction or composition criticism as practiced is analogous to exegeting a parable without knowing it *is* a parable, and without
an awareness of parables!"

48. E.g., W. R. Farmer, "The Problem of Christian Origins: A Pro-
grammatic Essay," in *Studies in the History and Text of the New
Testament*, B. L. Daniels and M. J. Suggs, eds. (Salt Lake City: Uni-
versity of Utah Press, 1967), p. 84 (on the basis of similar content);
G. Vermes, *Jesus the Jew* (London: Collins, 1973), p. 42; J. Z. Smith,
"Good News is No News: Aretalogy and Gospel," in *Christianity,
Judaism, and Other Greco-Roman Cults: Part One—New Testament*,
J. Neusner, ed. (Leiden: Brill, 1975), pp. 21–38; Dieter Georgi, "The
Records of Jesus in the Light of Ancient Accounts of Revered Men,"
SBL Seminar Papers, 1972, Vol. 2, 541–42 (Mark consciously presents
the record of Jesus in analogy to the vita of a philosopher). Roland
Frye, "A Literary Perspective for the Criticism of the Gospels," in *Jesus
and Man's Hope*, Vol. 2, pp. 207–11, 219, n. 28, says the gospels belong
to the genre of dramatic history along with the historical plays of
Shakespeare and G. B. Shaw and Plutarch's *Lives*. Dan O. Via, Jr.,
Kerygma and Comedy in the New Testament (Philadelphia: Fortress,
1975), p. 97, says, "Frye's suggestions ring true to me. . . ." From my
perspective, grouping Shakespeare, Shaw, and Plutarch together creates
more problems than it solves. John Drury, "What Are the Gospels?"
Expository Times, 87 (1976), 324–28, thinks Mark is a rough biography.

49. Moses Hadas and Morton Smith, *Heroes and Gods* (New York:
Harper & Row, 1965). Cf. also Moses Hadas, *Hellenistic Culture* (New
York: Columbia University Press, 1959), Chap. 13, especially pp.
172–77.

50. Moses Hadas and Morton Smith, *Heroes and Gods*, p. 3.

51. Morton Smith, "Prolegomena to a Discussion of Aretalogies,
Divine Men, the Gospels and Jesus," *JBL*, 90 (1971), 196.

52. The ambiguity of the term *aretalogy* in modern scholarship has
been pointed out by Paul J. Achtemeier, "Toward the Isolation of Pre-
Markan Miracle Catenae," *JBL*, 89 (1970), 266, n. 2.

53. Alexander Scobie, *Aspects of the Ancient Romance and Its Heritage* (Meisenheim am Glan: Anton Hain, 1969), pp. 20–29; Howard C.
Kee, "Aretalogy and Gospel," *JBL*, 92 (1973), 403.

54. Moses Hadas and Morton Smith, *Heroes and Gods*, p. 60.

55. Howard Clark Kee, "Aretalogy and Gospel," pp. 415–16.

56. This thesis is strongly argued by B. E. Perry, *The Ancient*

Romances (Berkeley: University of California Press, 1967), Part 1, "The Ideal Greek Romance of Love and Adventure."

57. Philip Shuler, "The Synoptic Gospels and the Problem of Genre," Ph.D. Dissertation, McMaster University, 1975.

58. For a discussion of these categories, see Chapter 4.

59. Raymond E. Brown, "Jesus and Elisha," *Perspective*, 12 (1971), 85–104.

60. Dom Aelred Baker, "Form and the Gospels," *Downside Review*, 88 (1970), 14–26; E. C. Hobbs, "Norman Perrin on Methodology in the Interpretation of Mark," in *Christology and a Modern Pilgrimage*, H. Dieter Betz, ed. (Society of Biblical Literature, 1971), p. 85; Meredith G. Kline, "The Old Testament Origins of the Gospel Genre," *Westminster Theological Journal*, 38 (1975), 1–27.

61. M. D. Goulder, *Midrash and Lection in Matthew* (London: SPCK, 1974).

62. *Ibid.*, p. 4.

63. *Ibid.*, pp. 33–34.

64. *Ibid.*, p. 34.

65. *Ibid.*, p. 171.

66. *Ibid.*, p. 172.

67. *Ibid.*, p. 152.

68. *Ibid.*, pp. 452–73, especially p. 455.

69. *Ibid.*, pp. 199–201.

70. The remarks that follow are indebted to the review by A. E. Harvey, *JTS*, n.s. 27 (1976), 188–95. Cf. also, J. D. M. Derrett, "Midrash in Matthew," *HeyJ* 16 (1975), 51–56.

2
Mythical Structure–1

The first foundation pillar for the contention of the critical consensus that the gospels are not biographies concerns myth. Bultmann argues that the canonical gospels present Jesus in terms of the Christ myth: in these Christian writings, Jesus is the divine Lord. The Graeco-Roman biographies according to Bultmann, however, treat human subjects in human terms. Since the gospels are mythical and the biographies are not, the gospels cannot belong to the biographical genre. In Chapter 1 it was suggested that this point implies a certain criterion for establishing genre connections. In order to say that the gospels belong to any ancient genre, it would be necessary to show that for that genre the outer form or structure was determined by myth.

In this chapter and the next we will focus on the question of outer form or structure as raised by Bultmann. In particular, we will ask whether or not ancient biography shared with the canonical gospels a structure determined by myth. Chapter 2 will treat the myth that controls the synoptic story and its relation to biography; Chapter 3 will move to the myth that orders the Fourth Gospel and its relation to biography. The aim of both chapters is to show that certain ancient biographies, like the canonical gospels, were ordered from a mythical point of view. In the present chapter our task is twofold: first, to describe the myth which controls the structure of the synoptics and to show its impact on Graeco-Roman literature, including biography; second to show the myth's influence on early Christianity, especially on the synoptic gospels. Let us turn to a description of the myth of the immortals in Mediterranean antiquity.

The concept of divinity in non-Christian antiquity near the be-

ginning of our era was complex.[1] It was possible to speak of the
two extremes, gods and men, and to mean by the former eternals
like Zeus/Jupiter in contrast to mere mortals.[2] In this case, divinity was far removed from humanity. It was also possible, however,
to speak of certain men as divine.

There were two separate categories of divinity into which such
men—spoken of as divine—might fall that are of special interest to
us here. On the one hand, certain men were believed in their
historical existence to have displayed the divine presence in some
special way and were hence regarded as *theioi andres*.[3] Opinions
differed over exactly what constituted the divine presence.[4]
Whereas some circles looked for it in a man's physical beauty or in
his prophetic utterances and miraculous feats,[5] others saw it manifest in extraordinary virtue and rationality.[6] There were also di-
vergent views about the origin or source of the divine presence.
Some looked to a supernatural conception, others to the conscious cultivation of virtue by a man born as other men normally
are.[7] At times these varying views both of what constituted the
divine presence and of the source of such divinity merged in a
synthetic portrayal of the *theios anēr*.[8] If a mortal possessed in an
unusual way that which was believed to constitute a sign of divine
presence, however conceived, he was regarded as a divine man.

On the other hand, a more select group of men were believed at
the end of their careers to have been taken up into heaven, to have
attained immortality, and to have received a status like that of the
eternal gods.[9] Such figures were designated immortals.[10] This
latter category of divinity is the primary concern of this chapter.

The Immortals

"Immortals" must be understood in the context of a distinction
between two types of divine beings, the eternals and the immortals.
This typology is mentioned at least as early as Herodotus, who
says that Hercules and Dionysus were gods who had a beginning to
their existence and had not existed eternally.[11] Herodotus' distinction between those deities that are eternal and those that are
immortal but have had a beginning was recognized and commented
on by Plutarch near the end of the first or the beginning of the

second century C.E.[12] It was, in fact, a widespread idea by the beginning of our era, two historians of the late first century B.C.E. reflecting the belief. Dionysius of Halicarnassus' *Roman Antiquities* refers to demigods such as Hercules and Asclepius, who are said to have ascended to heaven and to have obtained the same honors as the gods.[13] In Diodorus of Sicily the typology is clearly articulated and applied to his narrative's contents. Diodorus says:

> As regards the gods . . . men of ancient times have handed down to later generations two different conceptions: certain of the gods, they say, are eternal and imperishable. . . . But the other gods, we are told, were terrestrial beings who attained to immortal honor and fame because of their benefactions to mankind, such as Heracles, Dionysus, Aristaeus, and the others who were like them.[14]

In another context he comments:

> And besides these there are other gods, they say, who were terrestrial, having once been mortals, but who, by reason of their sagacity and the good services which they rendered to all men, attained immortality, some of them having even been kings in Egypt.[15]

Near the same time, the concept is developed elaborately in Philo's *Embassy to Gaius*, 77–114. Plutarch puts it concisely when he says that Apollo is not—

> from among those deities who were changed from mortals into immortals, like Heracles and Dionysus, whose virtues enabled them to cast off mortality and suffering; but he is one of those deities who are unbegotten and eternal, if we may judge by what the most ancient and wisest men have said on such matters.[16]

This typology retained its force at least into the third century C.E. where it is integral to part of Origen's polemic against Celsus.[17] Mediterranean antiquity drew a distinction between two kinds of deities: eternal beings like Zeus/Jupiter and immortals like Hercules and Dionysus.

The distinguishing marks of the immortals were: (1) the deity had originally been mortal, and (2) at the end of his career there occurred a transformation or ascension so that he obtained the same honors as the eternals. Since the second characteristic is crucial, whenever Mediterranean peoples spoke about the immortals constant in their description was the explicit or implicit "he was taken up into heaven." Some evidence of this ascent is usually given: either the ascent to heaven was witnessed[18] or there was no trace of physical remains.[19] That the absence of the hero's physical remains points properly to ascent to heaven is known because of (a) predictions/oracles during the hero's life that he would be taken up,[20] (b) a heavenly announcement at the end of his earthly career stating or implying that he had been taken up,[21] and (c) appearances of the hero to friends or disciples confirming his new status.[22] In addition, another feature frequently present in the description of the immortals is a reference to the man's being begotten by a god of a human mother, the usual procedure, or his being the child of a goddess and a human father.[23] Almost always, both the unusual circumstances concerning his birth and those relating to his passing are present. Occasionally, for whatever reason, if the reference to a supernatural begetting is missing,[24] the ascent into heaven is constant. When one spoke of an immortal in the Graeco-Roman world, therefore, he meant a mortal who had become a god, usually expressed in terms of an extraordinary birth (one of his parents was a deity) and ascension into heaven (witnessed to by such circumstances as there being no remains of his body to be found).

Originally the concept belonged to accounts of legendary or mythical figures of the distant past. Egyptian, Greek, and Roman examples are readily available. (1) *Egyptian*. Diodorus tells us, immediately after a reference to the typology of eternals and immortals,[25] that Osiris belongs to the second category.[26] Osiris was a king of Egypt, he says, who by reason of the magnitude of his benefactions received the gift of immortality with honor equal to that offered to the gods of heaven, the eternals. Moreover, there is one tradition which claimed that this Osiris was the offspring of a human daughter and Zeus. (2) *Greek*. Diodorus, in describing the Greek demigods, includes traditions about such figures as Dionysus, Hercules, Aristaeus, and Asclepius. (a) Dionysus was the son of Zeus and Semele, daughter of Cadmus, founder of Thebes. He became, however, one of the two demigods to be

accepted among the Olympians.[27]   (b) Hercules was the second
of the demigods deemed worthy of the name Olympian by Zeus.[28]
He was the son of Zeus and Alcmene, a daughter of Perseus.[29]
Zeus determined that after performing the twelve labors, Hercules
was to be given immortality.[30]   When at his death men looked for
his bones and found not a single one, they assumed, in accordance
with the oracle about his future, that he had passed from among
men into the company of the gods.[31]   Afterwards he was honored
with sacrifices both as a hero and as a god.[32]   Hera adopted him
as her son.[33]   (c) Aristaeus was the son of Apollo and the woman
Cyrene.   After dwelling in the region of Mount Haemus, he was
never again seen by men.   Assuming that he had been taken into
heaven, they made him the recipient of immortal honors.[34]   (d)
Asclepius was believed to have been the son of Apollo and either
Coronis or Arsinae,[35] and at the request of Apollo, Zeus placed
him among the stars.[36]   (3) *Roman.*   (a) Aeneas was believed to
have been the son of Venus.[37]   According to Dionysius of Halicarnassus, he was thought to have been translated to the gods when,
after a certain battle, his body was nowhere to be found.   Hence
the Latins built a shrine to him with the inscription: "To the father
and god of this place. . . ."[38]   (b) It was about Romulus that the
Roman traditions clustered in a special way.   They claimed he was
the son of Mars and a virgin, either Ilia or Rhea Silvia.[39]   His
great achievements led to the belief that when he disappeared, during a sudden darkening of the sun amidst a descending cloud, he
had been added to the number of the gods.[40]   This was witnessed
to by the fact that no portion of his body or fragment of his clothing
remained to be seen.[41]   This belief was reinforced by the claim of
one of his friends, Julius Proculus, that Romulus appeared to him
on the road and announced that he was to be worshiped as the god
Quirinus.[42]

The concept of immortals also made inroads into certain circles
of *Judaism* and attached itself to the figure of Moses.[43]   Although
there is a persistent rabbinic tradition that Moses did not die but
ascended to heaven,[44] the native home for the view of Moses'
bodily rapture was probably Hellenistic Judaism.[45]   Philo knew
traditions that understood Deuteronomy 34:6 to mean Moses was

translated.[46] His account of the end of Moses' career in his *Life of Moses* 2.288 reads like a description of an immortal's ascent to heaven.[47]

> Afterwards the time came when he had to make his pilgrimage from earth to heaven, and to leave this mortal life for immortality, summoned thither by the Father who resolved his twofold nature of soul and body into a single unity, transforming his whole being into mind, pure as the sunlight.[48]

Philo, however, protects himself against such an interpretation by including a reference to Moses' death and burial.[49]

In Josephus' *Antiquities* the account of Moses' end seems reminiscent of the "passing" of the two founders of the Roman race, Aeneas and Romulus.[50] We are told that a cloud suddenly descended upon him and that he disappeared in a ravine.[51] This, of course, echoes the usual "death/ascension" aspect of the mythology of the immortals. Josephus apparently tried to protect against such implications of this tradition because he immediately adds: "But he has written of himself in the sacred books that he died, for fear lest they should venture to say that by reason of his surpassing virtue he had gone back to the Deity."[52] This reading of Josephus is reinforced by his comment that when Moses was forty days in the mountain receiving the law, some said: "He had been taken back to the divinity."[53] Josephus, therefore, knew a Jewish tradition of the end of Moses' career that spoke of his passing in the same terms as those employed for the legendary heroes of other Mediterranean peoples. Even as he included the tradition shaped in this way, he explicitly rejected the interpretation of it in terms of the mythology of immortals. Though Philo and Josephus responded negatively, certain Jewish circles portrayed Moses in categories taken from the Mediterranean concept of the immortals.[54]

Egyptian, Greek, Roman, and Jewish evidence points to the belief in the existence of a certain category of deity, the immortals, alongside the eternals. These mythical and legendary figures were all benefactors of mankind: good kings, healers, strong men who used their might to conquer powers hostile to other men, those who introduced certain skills or goods into civilization, and great teachers. Their extraordinary lives were usually explained by their un-usual parentage;[55] their present status as divinities by their ascent to heaven.

Since this pattern was conventional in speech about many bene-factors of mankind from the distant past, it eventually attached itself to individuals of the not-too-distant past, mainly of two types: rulers and philosophers.[56] Among the rulers especially Alexander the Great and Augustus were so treated; among the philosophers Empedocles, Apollonius of Tyana, and Peregrinus. In attaching itself to clearly historical personages, this mythology affected the literary genres of history and biography. To the influence of the concept in non-Christian antiquity we now turn.

Immortals in History, Biography, and Satire

The motif of immortals was attached first to rulers from the not-too-distant past. Alexander the Great is treated in this way both in history and in biography. Though there is a real question about the genre of Arrian's *Anabasis Alexandri*, it most likely should be regarded as a fusion of both history and biography.[57] Arrian's treatment of Alexander in the second century C.E. is rationalistic and avoids the romantic elements in his career. Reflecting his distaste for such beliefs, Arrian attempted to expose the reality of the situation. He says:

> One writer has not even shrunk from the statement that Alexander, perceiving that he could not survive, went to throw himself into the Euphrates, so that he might disappear from the world and leave behind the tradition more credible to posterity *that his birth was of the gods and that to the gods he passed*; but Roxane his wife saw that he was going out, and when she prevented him he cried aloud that she then grudged him everlasting fame as having been truly born a god.[58] (Italics added)

This tells us both that such a concept existed in traditions attached to Alexander and that Arrian discounted it. Nevertheless, he is forced to conclude: "And so not even I can suppose that a man quite beyond all other men was born without some divine influ-ence."[59]

In the romantic biography of Pseudo-Callisthenes the motif of such a birth is clear. We hear how Olympias was made pregnant by a god, Ammon of Egypt. Philip was convinced that her pregnancy was socially acceptable, even though he was away from home, because of a dream in which he was told that it was due to a god. At the end of the narrative, in connection with the death of Alexander, we hear that there was darkness, that a star and an eagle were seen falling from heaven, that a statue of Zeus was shaken, and that the star and eagle were seen going back to heaven carrying a brilliant star. Such a description of Alexander's ascent to heaven was regarded as the answer to his prayer to Zeus: "And if it be thy will, receive me too in heaven, as the third mortal."[60] By the beginning of our era, therefore, the mythology of immortals with its themes of miraculous conception and ascent to heaven had become attached to the figure of Alexander the Great in both Graeco-Roman history and biography.[61]

The mythology of immortals also attached itself to Augustus in historical and biographical writings of the Roman Empire. In Dio Cassius' *Roman History* the normal chain of social and political events in Rome's history is broken both at the birth and at the death of Augustus by the inclusion of the myth. In Book 45 the narrative about his birth asserts the belief that he was engendered by Apollo;[62] in Book 56 the narrative of his death tells of Augustus' being declared immortal in the presence of priests and sacred rites. There is, furthermore, also a reference to the tradition that Numerius Atticus, a senator and ex-praetor, swore he had seen Augustus ascending to heaven after the manner of Romulus and Proculus.[63] It is clear, from the way both birth and ascension themes are related, that Dio was hostile to them. That he included them, nevertheless, testifies to their prevalence in the tradition relating to Augustus.[64]

This mythology also colors the Alexandrian-type biography of Augustus composed by Suetonius. As Suetonius tells it, Atia came to the temple of Apollo and fell asleep. A serpent glided up to her and went away. In the tenth month after that Augustus was born.[65] He was, therefore, regarded as the son of Apollo. Suetonius also relates the tradition about the ex-praetor who took an oath that he had seen the form of the emperor on its way up to heaven.[66] Augustus, like Alexander the Great, was depicted in histories and biographies in terms of the concept of the immortals.

The same mythology was also used to describe certain philosophers from the not-too-distant past. The Pythagorean philosopher Empedocles (484–424 B.C.E.) is depicted by Diogenes Laertius both as a teacher and as a worker of miracles like the later Apollonius of Tyana. Though there is no account of divine parentage for him, Laertius relates a purportedly ancient tradition in connection with his death which shows that in some circles Empedocles was thought of in terms of the category of immortals. According to Heraclides of Pontus, says Laertius, after an evening meal or party with his friends, Empedocles disappeared and was nowhere to be found. One of the company claimed to have heard a voice from heaven calling the philosopher. Hence it was believed that he was taken up into heaven and was now a god.[67] That Laertius then cites other explanations of Empedocles' passing which attempt to discredit the first one shows the controversial context within which lives of philosophers circulated in antiquity.[68] Some circles, doubtless Pythagorean, placed Empedocles among the immortals.

In Philostratus' *Life of Apollonius of Tyana* the mythology of immortals is found complete. The birth traditions relate that Apollonius' mother had a vision just before she gave birth in which a god of Egypt told her she would give birth to himself.[69] Later the people call Apollonius a "son of Zeus."[70] The versions of his passing are diverse, but one clearly comes from such a mentality. The story goes that Apollonius entered the temple of Athene, whereupon a chorus of maidens was heard singing from within: "Hasten thou from earth, hasten thou to Heaven, hasten;" in other words: "Do thou go upwards from earth."[71] Afterwards his remains could not be found. Then he is said to have appeared to a fervent disciple and through him taught men further, even though he had already passed from this earth.[72]

When, in the histories and biographies of the Graeco-Roman world, the mythology of the immortals was included in the description of the careers of historical rulers and philosophers the intent was to speak about the significance of the individual. It is hardly

accidental that this concept was used of precisely those personages
—rulers and philosophers—who in antiquity were often associated
with communities which constituted a cult for the divine figure.[73]

The knowledge and use of the mythology of the immortals apparently became so widespread, and loosely applied, that it became the
object of satire. Satirical treatments of the myth can be found in
Seneca and Lucian. Seneca, in *The Pumpkinification of Claudius*,
gives vent to his feelings about the ridiculous extremes to which the
whole process had been carried. The fact that Julia Drusilla, sister
of Emperor Gaius Caligula, was deified at her death in 38 C.E. at
Gaius' insistence was scandalous to Seneca. Even Livius Geminius
swore before the Senate that he had seen her going up to heaven.[74]
Now there was Claudius. In a heavenly debate over whether to
grant Claudius the status of deity, Seneca has one heavenly speaker
complain: "Once . . . it was a great thing to become a god; now you
have made it a . . . farce. . . . I propose that from this day forward
the godhead be given to none of those who eat the fruits of the
earth, or whom mother earth doth nourish."[75]

In *The Parliament of the Gods*, Lucian has Momus complain to
Zeus about the large number of gods that have been allowed into
heaven such as Dionysus, Asclepius, and Hercules.[76] Lucian's
satire is most telling in the *Passing of Peregrinus*. Here he tells the
story of Peregrinus who, after his rejection by the Christians for his
transgressions, took up philosophy and fell to abusing everyone,
especially the emperor. When no one would pay him attention any
longer, he proceeded, imitating Hercules, to burn himself on a pyre
at a festival. Before he died in the fire, however, he manufactured
myths and repeated certain óracles to the effect that he was to
become a guardian spirit, apparently coveting altars and expecting
to be imaged in gold. He also appointed ambassadors from among
his comrades to be sent out with the good tidings. Lucian claims
to have been there at the spectacle which took place outside the
city. On his way back, he says that in jest he told some people a
wild story.

When the pyre was kindled and Proteus flung himself bodily in, a
great earthquake first took place, accompanied by a bellowing of

the ground, and then a vulture, flying out of the midst of the
flames, went off to Heaven, saying, in human speech, with a loud
voice: "I am through with the earth; *to Olympus I fare*."[77] (Italics
added)

When he got back to the city, Lucian relates, he met a grey-haired
man with a dignified air telling that he had just beheld Proteus in
white raiment walking about cheerfully in the Portico of the Seven
Voices. The old man also claimed to have seen the vulture flying
up out of the pyre.[78] Lucian closes by expressing his fears that
honors will be heaped upon Peregrinus partly because of his joke.
Though the divine parentage theme is missing, the description of
Peregrinus' death indicates that Lucian is poking fun at the widespread tendency to class individuals of the immediate historical past
among the immortals. Only that which has been carried to excess
can be the object of this type of ridicule.

What is constitutive for the status of an immortal? The protagonist is first of all a mortal—though perhaps so extraordinary as to
be regarded in some sense divine during his lifetime, but mortal
nonetheless.[79] At the end of his career, by the decree or act of
some eternal, he is taken up into heaven, becomes immortal, and
takes his place in the pantheon of gods.[80]

The Relation of the Immortals to THEIOI ANDRES

With a sharpened awareness of what was constitutive for the
mythology of immortals in antiquity, we may now ask about its
relation to the conception of divine men near the beginning of our
era. On the one hand, it is important to reiterate that we are
dealing with two different ideas.[81] Not every *theios anēr* was
believed to have become an immortal. Porphyry's *Life of Pythagoras*, for example, describes Pythagoras as a divine man but not as
an immortal. There were, furthermore, attempts in some circles to
keep the two conceptions separate. Josephus in the *Antiquities*
could use the one and repress the other as is clearly seen in his
treatment of Moses. He can refer to Moses as a *theion andra*,
attempting to demonstrate Moses' surpassing virtue. This conception of divinity was serviceable for the Judaism of Josephus, but the

myth of immortals, as our earlier discussion showed, was not.[82] Philo, in addition to the categories "eternals/immortals," knew the concept *theios anēr*. He says that absolute sinlessness belongs to God alone, or possibly to a divine man (θείου ἀνδρός). In his *Life of Moses*, he says Moses was named god (θεός) and king of the whole nation.[83] In himself and his life Moses displayed a godlike work (θεοειδὲς ἔργον) for all to see, a model for those willing to copy it. When Philo comes to the end of Moses' career, however, we have seen that he refuses to interpret it as the ascent of an immortal. Both Josephus and Philo find suitable that variety of the concept of *theios anēr* in which divine presence is understood in terms of virtue, though neither approves of the mythology of the immortals.

It was, however, inevitable that these two originally different conceptions of divinity would sometimes merge, the one complementing the other. There were certainly similarities between them. Accounts of both *theioi andres* and immortals, for example, sometimes appealed to a supernatural parentage as an explanation for the extraordinary life of the protagonist.[84] The actual basis for any complementary association of these two notions of divinity, however, occurred whenever the nature of the earthly career of the hero was understood in terms of the mythology of immortals. The lives of those who became immortals were virtuous.[85] They were benefactors of men. As Diodorus puts it, the terrestrial beings gained immortal honor and fame "because of their benefactions to mankind. . . ."[86] Elsewhere he says it was "by reason of their sagacity and the good services which they rendered to all men" that they attained immortality.[87] Dio Chrysostom says that Zeus honored Hercules "because of his virtue." Elsewhere he makes the same point about all of the demigods.[88] Here is an explicit point of contact with the idea of *theios anēr* in most of its forms.[89] Whenever the two conceptions of divinity did merge, the result was a picture of some mortal functioning in his historical existence as a *theios anēr* who was a benefactor of men and who at the end of his life was taken up into heaven, attaining the status of an immortal.

An example of the result of such a merger of the two conceptions of divinity is found in Philostratus' *Life of Apollonius of Tyana*. The *Life* depicts Apollonius as a *theios anēr* (e.g., 1:2; 2:17; 2:40; 5:24; 7:21; 7:38; 8:5; 8:7) whose divinity is manifest primarily in his wisdom and virtue (cf. 1:2; 7:7:[ii], [iii], [iv]; 8:7:[7]).[90] Philostratus thereby protects the philosopher from the charge of having been a magician, as was claimed by Euphrates during his lifetime and by Moeragenes after his death.[91]

Philostratus' major source, the memoirs of Damis, ends at 8:28 of the *Life*. He tells us that the memoirs did not deal with the manner in which Apollonius died, *"if he did actually die"* (8:29, italics added).[92] His caution in speaking about the end of Apollonius' career is necessitated by the fact that Philostratus adds material from another source which depicts the saint's end in terms of an immortal (8:30), an account followed by the statement: "no one ventured to dispute that he was immortal" (ἀθάνατος). Then comes an appearance to a disciple in which further teaching is given. The result of the addition of this material to Philostratus' revision of Damis' memoirs is a portrayal of Apollonius as a wise and virtuous *theios anēr* during his earthly career and as an immortal at his end. A merger has taken place here between two originally distinct views of divinity.

A less perfect synthesis of the two conceptions is found in Diogenes Laertius' treatment of the life of Empedocles. One tradition of Empedocles' end used by Laertius, we have noted, portrayed it as the passing of an immortal, though Laertius also included others that tended to discredit the first (*Lives of Eminent Philosophers* 8:67–68). It is also true that the career of Empedocles is cast, in part at least, in terms of a divine man. In 8:62 (cf. also 8:66), Empedocles says, "I go about among you an immortal god (θεὸς ἄμβροτος), no more a mortal (οὐκέτι θνητός)." He says this as people look to him for wisdom, oracles, and healing. That this was understood in the time of Laertius to be the claim of a *theios anēr* is clear from its use in Philostratus' *Life of Apollonius*. Philostratus' intent is to portray Apollonius as a divine man of the same type as Pythagoras, Empedocles, and Plato.[93] In this context the line from Empedocles, also found in Laertius, is cited. In Laertius' life of

Empedocles, the two conceptions of divinity, *theios anēr* and immortals, exist side by side. Both were required for some people in antiquity adequately to speak of this philosopher.

A final example of such a synthesis is from Pseudo-Lucian. In *The Cynic* 13, Hercules is called a divine man (θεῖον ἄνδρα) and is said rightly to be considered a god (θεόν). Only a failure to recognize the original difference between the conceptions of a divine man and an immortal could cloud the distinction here.[94] The statement which follows about Hercules leaving the realm of men (ἐξ ἀνθρώπων ἀπῆλθεν) makes it certain that for Hercules to be considered a god means he is believed to have become an immortal. Here again the two views of divinity merge.

The Immortals and Early Christianity

Having clarified a basic pattern present at the beginning of our era in the understanding of divinity in the Mediterranean world, we must now explore its twofold relationship to early Christian thought.

Certain early Christians regarded the immortals as demonic imitations of Christ. Justin Martyr, for example, was not only aware of the traditions about the immortals but also of the remarkable similarities between such figures and Jesus Christ. Indeed, he uses these resemblances for his apologetic ends. The Christians' assertions about Jesus Christ, he argues, propose nothing new or different from that which pagans say about the immortals, e.g., Asclepius, Hercules, Dionysus, and the Dioscuri.[95] If Christians assert that Christ was born of a virgin, that he was crucified, died, rose from the dead, and ascended into heaven, this is nothing new or different from what pagans say about the so-called sons of Jupiter and certain emperors.[96] Granting these similarities between the Christians' savior and the pagans' immortals, why should Christian belief seem incredible to pagans?

Justin's Christology did not utilize the mythology of immortals as its central conceptual tool. It was imperative, therefore, for him to explain the similarities between Jesus and the immortals of pagan tradition. He did this by claiming that the Devil counterfeited Christian realities in the fictions circulated among the pagans.[97] These pagan myths were first related through the instigation of evil demons "who strive for nothing else than to alienate men from God their Creator and from Christ. . . ."[98] The demons did not grasp clearly the meaning of what they heard from the prophets. Like erring men, they mimicked what was said of Christ. So, for example, when the pagans say that Dionysus was born of Jupiter's union with Semele and that after he died, he arose again and ascended into heaven, this is due to the Devil's having imitated the prophecy of Jacob in Genesis 49:10–11.[99] Or when Asclepius is presented in pagan lore as raising the dead to life and curing all diseases, this is a devilish imitation of the prophecy in Isaiah 35:1–7.[100] It is only a short distance from this conviction that Jesus is the true reality of which the immortals are only demonic imitations to an explicit employment of the mythology of immortals as a conceptual tool in Christology.

In contrast to the position taken by Justin, then, there are indications that some early Christians did think about Christ in terms of the mythology of the immortals. Three elements warrant this conclusion.

1. Recent research has described the Christology of Hellenistic Jewish Christianity in terms of four constitutive elements:[101] (a) From the moment of his resurrection/exaltation/ascension Jesus became Lord, Christ, Son of God and now actively reigns in heaven (Acts 2:36; 13:33; Rom. 1:3–4). Of the four elements, this is primary; (b) By means of traditions about his virginal conception, Jesus' earthly sonship is expressed in terms of the modified Hellenistic Jewish concept of the divine man;[102] (c) Nevertheless, Jesus is qualified for the Messianic office not by mere physical descent, but by his virtuous treatment of the sick and suffering (e.g., Mark 10:46–52); (d) There is on occasion an undeveloped concept of an inactive preexistence of the Son (cf. Mark 12:6).

The average Mediterranean man-in-the-street who was confronted by such a christological pattern would immediately grasp its intent. Jesus, he would assume, is being portrayed as an immortal.[103] Jesus' ascent into the heavens, like that of the other immortals, is constitutive for his new status. Thereby he begins a new type of existence different from that of mortal men. Jesus' historical career radiates virtue and is beneficial to men. This uniqueness can only be explained by a supernatural conception.[104] Only the occasional presence in Hellenistic Jewish Christian Christology of a concept of inactive preexistence presents a problem. A solution may be found in the Romulus tradition where the same type of concept of preexistence is present.

Julius Proculus, in Plutarch's narrative, claims to have seen Romulus after the king's departure. Romulus, he reported, said to him:

> It was the pleasure of the gods, O Proculus, *from whom I came* (ἐκεῖθεν ὄντας), that I should be with mankind only a short time, and that after founding a city destined to be the greatest on earth for empire and glory, *I should dwell again in heaven* (αὖθις οἰκεῖν οὐρανόν). . . . And I will be your propitious deity, Quirinus.[105]
> (Italics added)

These words appear in the context of Romulus' becoming an immortal. Here is the same notion of preexistence that one finds in Hellenistic Jewish Christian Christology. A Mediterranean person who heard Jesus depicted in this way would find it difficult to avoid understanding him in terms of the mythology of immortals. Furthermore, it is likely that those who formulated this christological pattern perceived him in this way.

Though the constitutive elements in Hellenistic Jewish Christian Christology and in the Mediterranean mythology of immortals are the same, the pattern when applied to Jesus would be different in at least two significant ways.[106] First, the Christian pattern would speak also of a parousia of Christ (1 Thess. 1:9–10). This would be an inheritance from the earlier Christian tradition. Second, the context for the Christian pattern would be the exclusive claim, "There is one Lord" (1 Cor. 8:6). Nevertheless, the general exaltation to heaven/virtuous life/supernatural conception of the mythology of immortals would be the beachhead in some circles on which the Christian proclamation of Jesus would make its first inroads. The Christology of Hellenistic Jewish Christianity seems clearly indebted to the concept of the immortals.

2. Since some early Christians did conceptualize Jesus in terms of the mythology of immortals, it seems inevitable that in such circles

the Jesus traditions would be affected by this mentality. Without making a judgment about their ultimate origins, one must note that certain materials have a natural *Sitz im Leben* in this christological context. In a cult celebrating the exaltation of Jesus as Lord, Christ, Son of God, an *ascension story* with a clear-cut function would be predictable. In some circles, the ascent of an immortal was believed to have been witnessed.[107] In other circles where the ascent of the immortal was inferred, an *empty tomb tradition*[108] and *stories of appearances*[109] would function appropriately.

3. More significant for our purposes is the influence of the mythology of the immortals on certain gospels taken as wholes. The myth ordered the synoptic story of Jesus, giving these three gospels their basic structure. This influence is seen at its fullest in Luke-Acts where we find a supernatural conception (Luke 1:35) followed by a virtuous life. According to Acts 2:36 (cf. 13:33), it is by virtue of his exaltation that Jesus becomes Lord, Christ, Son of God. Luke gives a synthetic portrayal of Jesus becoming Lord. On the one hand, his passing from mortal to immortal is attested by the absence of Jesus' physical remains (Luke 24:1–11 [12]), reinforced both by appearances to friends and disciples in which further instruction is given (Luke 24:13–49; Acts 1:1–5) and by predictions made during his life (Luke 9:22; 18:32–33—to which specific reference is made in 24:6–8). On the other hand, Jesus' ascent through a cloud is witnessed by the Galileans (Acts 1:9–11). There is no way a Mediterranean man could have missed this as a portrayal of Jesus in the mythology of the immortals. That Luke-Acts is so influenced is noteworthy because it is in this gospel that the parallels between Jesus and the ancient philosophers are the greatest.[110] If the converts in Luke's church came from the Graeco-Roman world where philosophers were sometimes described as divine men who became immortals, then the Lucan picture of Jesus is intelligible.

The impact of this mentality is also evident in Matthew. Here again we meet a supernatural conception followed by a virtuous life. According to Matthew 28:18, it is because he has passed from mortal to immortal that Jesus now has a new status as Lord. The evidence of his ascent into the heavens consists of the absence of his physical remains together with the now familiar duo: appearances in which instruction is given (28:9–10, 16–20), and predictions stemming from Jesus' earthly career. (16:21; 17:22–23; 20:18–19). Again, the way a Hellenistic person would have interpreted this portrayal is virtually certain. That Matthew is so influenced by the mythology of the immortals is significant because it is in this gospel that the parallels between Jesus and Moses are most pronounced. Though the resemblances between the Evangelist's description of Jesus and Josephus's depiction of Moses are striking, the differences between them are at the points of divine parentage and the status of the hero as an object of worship at the end of his career. These are precisely the points that some Jews made in going beyond Josephus to describe Moses as an immortal. If the Christian converts in Matthew's church came from such circles as these, then the First Gospel's portrayal of Jesus is meaningful.

In Mark there are no narratives dealing with a supernatural conception. This is not decisive since Laertius' *Life of Empedocles* contained no such account yet ended with an ascent tradition. His remains were nowhere to be found. This is precisely what we find in Mark. There is an empty tomb story which has, of late, properly been recognized as an ascent tradition. Connected with it are the predictable corollaries: predictions during Jesus' lifetime (8:31; 9:31; 10:32–33), and a reference to an appearance (16:7).[111] A Hellenistic reader confronted with this structure would have understood the gospel in much the same terms as he would have used in interpreting Laertius' *Life of Empedocles*. Here is a *theios anēr* about whom the claim is made that he became an immortal at the end of his career.

It would seem, therefore, that early Christians were aware of the Mediterranean myth of the immortals and utilized it in one way or another in their proclamation of Jesus. When they employed this myth in the gospels of Matthew, Mark, and Luke-Acts as a principle by which to order the Jesus materials, they were doing what pagan and Jewish writers had already done and were doing. The sweeping statement that Graeco-Roman biographies were not mythical is inaccurate. The mythology of the immortals was used by some as the frame for their story—as do the synoptic gospels.

Two objections must be faced at this point. The first is that the biographies of rulers and philosophers which are controlled by the myth of immortals are too late to serve as parallels to the canonical gospels. Arrian, Pseudo-Callisthenes, Suetonius, Diogenes Laertius, Philostratus, and Lucian all belong to the second and third centuries of our era. (1) Most of the extant biographies from Mediterranean antiquity are, to be sure, from the time of the Roman Empire,[112] great numbers of pre-Christian biographies being either lost or known to us only in fragments. Recognizing this fact conditions one's understanding of the date of these Lives. Virtually all the Lives we could cite would be this late. (2) Some of the writers cited indicate they are using earlier material. Arrian, Suetonius, and Diogenes Laertius specifically refer to the prior existence of the myth of immortals in the accounts of Alexander, Augustus, and Empedocles. The phenomenon was earlier than the authors, that is, prior to the second century. The Jewish evidence indicates the practice existed in those circles at least by the early first century and probably before that. (3) Such a practice of telling a notable man's life in terms of the myth of immortals was entertained as a possibility by Isocrates in his *Evagoras* (21, 72), but rejected. Taken together, these three facts answer the first objection. That most of our extant biographies structured in terms of the myth of immortals are from the second and third centuries does not mean such a practice was late. Their roots were in pre-Christian times.

The second question concerns whether or not the presence or absence of myth is determinative for genre decisions. The myth of immortals, for example, can be present in (e.g., Suetonius' *Augustus*) or absent from (e.g., Nicolaus of Damascus' *Life of Augustus*) biographies, as well as present in both history (e.g., Dio Cassius' section on Augustus) and biography. The answer here must be that taken in isolation myth is not determinative of genre. It is only in conjunction with other factors, such as function, that it can be helpful in genre decisions. It is now necessary to turn to the myth which controls the Fourth Gospel and to ask about its relation to the biographical tradition.

NOTES

1. Morton. Smith, "Prolegomena to a Discussion of Aretalogies, Divine Men, the Gospels and Jesus," *JBL* 90 (1971), 181–84. My concern here is limited to conceptions of divinity near the beginning of our era. It focuses on the concept of the immortals because this is the concern of such ancient writers as Diodorus of Sicily. It brings in the *theios anēr* concept as an auxiliary concern because of its importance in current discussions in New Testament study, e.g., Paul J. Achtemeier, "Gospel Miracle Traditions and the Divine Man," *Int* 26 (1972), 174–97.

2. E.g., Lucian, *Zeus Catechized.* "On How Many Heads One Should Praise a God," by the second-century rhetorician Alexander, begins with a reference to the philosophic view that god is unbegotten and not susceptible of destruction. Cf. A. D. Nock, *Conversion* (London: Oxford, 1933), p. 231.

3. Hans Windisch, *Paulus und Christus* (Leipzig: J. C. Hinrichs'sche, 1934); Ludwig Bieler, ΘΕΙΟΣ ANHP, 2 vols. (Wien: Oskar Höfels, 1935–36).

4. David L. Tiede, *The Charismatic Figure as Miracle Worker*, SBL Dissertation Series, 1. (Missoula, Montana: Society of Biblical Literature, 1972).

5. E.g., Plato, *Meno* 99 B–D; Dio Chrysostom, *Discourse* 33:4; Lucian, *Alexander the False Prophet* 12–13; Philostratus, *Life of Apollonius* 7:38; Origen, *Against Celsus* 7:9.

6. E.g., Cicero, *About the Ends of Goods and Evils* 1:5:14; *Tusculan Disputations* 1:21:48; Lucretius, 5:8–10; 5:25–50; 1:729–734; Seneca, *On Providence* 6:6; *Epistle* 73:14–16; 31:11; 41:1; Plutarch, *On the Fortunes of Alexander* 331 A; Epictetus, 1:9:22–26; Dio Chrysostom, *Discourse* 69:1; Josephus, *Antiquities* 3.7,7§180.

7. Dio Chrysostom, *Discourse* 4:18–23, has Diogenes tell Alexander of the two criteria by which a man was regarded as divine, i.e., a son of Zeus: (1) being conceived supernaturally, (2) being self-controlled and noble. Diogenes then says: "If, however, you are cowardly and love luxury and have a servile nature, then you are in no way related to the gods. . . ." (cf. also 69:1) This constitutes Dio's critique of (1) in the name of (2). For another statement of the second criterion, cf. Lucian, *Demonax* 7, 63. For the first criterion, cf. Lucretius, 1:729–33, who says of Empedocles: "he seems hardly to be born of mortal stock." The same thing could be said of certain rabbis. Cf. b. Nid. 13a; also

Jacob Neusner, *History of the Jews in Babylonia* (Leiden: Brill, 1968), Vol. 3, p. 107. According to S. J. Case, *Experience with the Supernatural in Early Christian Times* (New York: Century, 1929), p. 129, another, less common, explanation of a divine man's distinctiveness was reincarnation (e.g., Pindar, *Threnoi*, Fragment 113; Vergil, *Aeneid* 6:756–76). Justin seems to be aware of and involved in the debates over what constitutes the true *theios anēr* in *1 Apology* 22, when he says: "even if he (Jesus) were only a man by common generation, he is because of his wisdom, worthy to be called Son of God."

8. Porphyry's *Life of Pythagoras* is a good example. Cf. Seneca, *On the Happy Life* 26:8–27:1 (also Tiede, *Charismatic Figure*, p. 59).

9. That is, he is not only immortal but also rules. Cf. Seneca, *Hercules Oetaeus* 1996–1997, who speaks of Hercules now reigning in power.

10. The terminology is complex. The lines between demigods, heroes, and immortals are blurred. This is true both for the classical period and the hellenistic age. I use *immortals* here to refer to those humans who become deities by virtue of their ascent to heaven at the end of their lives. I use *demigod* only when the individual has a supernatural parentage. Not all demigods became immortals. I avoid the term *hero* in any technical sense since heroes constituted a group larger than those who became immortals. On this problem, cf. Erwin Rohde, *Psyche* (London: Routledge & Kegan Paul, 1925) pp. 117–32, 141, n. 23; A. D. Nock, "The Cult of Heroes," *HTR* 37 (1944), 141–74.

11. Herodotus, *Histories* 2:43; 2:145–46.

12. Plutarch, "On the Malice of Herodotus" 13 (*Moralia*).

13. Dionysius of Halicarnassus, *Roman Antiquities* 7:72:13.

14. Diodorus of Sicily, *Library of History* 6:1.

15. *Ibid.*, 1:13.

16. Plutarch, "Pelopidas" 16.

17. Origen, *Against Celsus* 3:22.

18. In general, cf. Justin, *1 Apology* 21; for Augustus, cf. Suetonius, *Augustus* 100, and Dio Cassius, 56:46; for Claudius, cf. Seneca, *Pumpkinification of Claudius*; for Alexander the Great, cf. Pseudo-Callisthenes, *Alexander Romance*; for Peregrinus, cf. Lucian, *The Passing of Peregrinus* 39–40.

19. For Hercules, cf. Diodorus of Sicily, 4:38:4–5; for Aristaeus, cf. Diodorus, 4:81–82; for Romulus, cf. Plutarch, "Romulus," 27; for Aeneas, cf. Dionysius of Halicarnassus, 1:64:4–5; for Empedocles, cf. Diogenes Laertius, *Lives of Eminent Philosophers* 8:67–68; for Apollon-

ius, cf. Philostratus, *Life of Apollonius*, 8:30.

20. So Hercules (Diodorus, 4:10:7); Peregrinus (Lucian, *The Passing of Peregrinus* 27); Alexander the Great (Pseudo-Callisthenes, *Alexander Romance* 3:24, 30).

21. So Empedocles (Laertius, *Lives* 8:67–68); Apollonius (Philostratus, *Life* 8:30); Peregrinus (Lucian, *Passing* 39).

22. So Romulus (Cicero, *The Republic* 2:10; *Laws* 1:1:3; Plutarch, "Romulus," 28; Tertullian, *Apology* 21); Apollonius (Philostratus, *Life* 8:31).

23. (a) Those with a deity for a father: Hercules (Diodorus, 4:9:1); Asclepius (Cicero, *On the Nature of the Gods* 3:22; Ovid, *Metamorphoses* 2:600–610); Dionysus (Diodorus, 4:2:1–4); Castor and Pollux (*Homeric Hymns* 32; Ovid, *Metamorphoses* 6:109); Romulus (Plutarch, "Romulus," 2). (b) Those with a deity for a mother: Aeneas (Ovid, *Metamorphoses* 14:588).

24. E.g., in the cases of Empedocles in Laertius' account (though Lucretius, 1:729–33, apparently knows of a supernatural birth) and of Peregrinus (Lucian, *Passing*).

25. Diodorus, *Library of History* 1:13.

26. *Ibid.*, 1:20, 23.

27. *Ibid.*, 4:2:1; cf. also Ovid, *Metamorphoses* 3:259–273.

28. Diodorus, *Library of History* 4:15:1.

29. *Ibid.*, 4:9:1.

30. *Ibid.*, 4:9:5.

31. *Ibid.*, 4:38:4–5.

32. *Ibid.*, 4:39:1; 5:76.

33. *Ibid.*, 4:39:2.

34. *Ibid.*, 4:81–82.

35. *Ibid.*, 4:71:1; cf. also *Homeric Hymn to Asclepius*; Pindar's *Third Pythian Ode*; Ovid, *Metamorphoses* 2:600–655; Cicero, *On the Nature of the Gods* 3:22; Pausanius, 2:26:4–5 (6); 3:26:4.

36. Cicero, *On the Nature of the Gods* 3:22:57.

37. Ovid, *Metamorphoses* 14:588.

38. Dionysius of Halicarnassus, *Roman Antiquities* 1:64:4–5.

39. Dionysius of Halicarnassus, 1:77:2; Cicero, *The Republic* 1:41; 2:2; Ovid, *Metamorphoses* 14:805–828; 15:862–63; Plutarch, "Romulus," 2; Lucius Annaeus Florus, 1:1.

40. Cicero, *The Republic* 2:10; 6:21; Livy, 1:16; Plutarch, "Romulus," 27; Florus, 1:1.

41. Plutarch, "Romulus," 27; Cicero, *Laws* 1:1:3; Livy, 1:16; Florus, 1:1.

42. Plutarch, "Romulus," 28. From the hostility with which Plutarch speaks, it is clear that the tradition assumed that Romulus ascended *bodily* into heaven.

43. It helps our perspective if we note the view of Moses put forward by the Hellenistic Jewish apologist Artapanus. He says of Moses: (1) He was the teacher of Orpheus (Eusebius, *P.E.* 9:27:4). Since Orpheus is said to have transferred the birthplace of Osiris to Thebes (Diodorus of Sicily, 1:23), Artapanus's claim makes Moses responsible, indirectly at least, for both Greek culture and the shape of an Egyptian cult; (2) he was called Musaeus by the Greeks (Eusebius, *P.E.* 9:27:3). Since Musaeus was equivalent to the Egyptian Hermes-Thoth, this claim is tantamount to making Moses into one of the gods of Egypt (Brian Colless, "Divine Education," *Numen* 17 [1970], 120); (3) he was regarded by the Egyptian priests as worthy of being honored like a god. Indeed, he was called Hermes (Eusebius, *P.E.* 9:27:6). Hellenistic Jews who went this far would have had no problems with a portrayal of Moses as an immortal.

44. Wayne A. Meeks, *The Prophet-King* (Leiden: Brill, 1967) pp. 209–211; Louis Ginzberg, *The Legends of the Jews* (Philadelphia: Jewish Publication Society of America, 1959) Vol. 6, p. 161; J. Jeremias, *TDNT*, Vol. 4, pp. 854–55.

45. Jeremias, *TDNT*, Vol. 4, p. 854.

46. Philo, *Sacrifices of Abel and Cain*, 3:8–10. Cf. Meeks, *Prophet-King*, p. 124; Ginzberg, *Legends*, Vol. 6, p. 142.

47. Henry Chadwick, "St. Paul and Philo of Alexandria," *BJRL* 48 (1966), 301.

48. As found in the Loeb Classical Library, Vol. 2, p. 288.

49. *Ibid.*, p. 291. Ginzberg, *Legends*, Vol. 6, p. 152, n. 904, thinks that when the *Testament of Moses* 1:15 and Pseudo-Philo, *Biblical Antiquities*, 19–20d stress that Moses was buried in a public place it is to combat the view that he did not die but was translated to heaven.

50. Introduction to the *Antiquities*, in The Loeb Classical Library, Vol. 4, p. ix.

51. *Antiquities* 4.8, 48§326.

52. *Ibid.* That Josephus is here taking issue with the speculation that Moses was translated, cf. Ginzberg, *Legends*, Vol. 6, pp. 152, 161; Jeremias, *TDNT*, Vol. 4, pp. 854–55; Eduard Schweizer, *The Good*

News according to Mark (Richmond: John Knox, 1970), p. 182.

53. *Antiquities*, 3.5, 7§96. R. H. Charles interprets Josephus differently. From the existing Greek fragments he reconstructed a Jewish document, the *Assumption of Moses*, which is different from the so-called Latin *Assumption* (actually the *Testament of Moses*) in his *Apocrypha and Pseudepigrapha* (Oxford: Clarendon, 1913), Vol. 2, p. 408. It is apparently the former document from which Clement of Alexandria draws in telling us that when Moses was taken up to heaven, Joshua and Caleb saw Moses double: one Moses with the angels, the other on the mountains being buried in their ravines (*Miscellanies*, 6:15. Cf. J. D. Purvis, "Samaritan Traditions on the Death of Moses," in *Studies on the Testament of Moses*, G. W. E. Nickelsburg, Jr., ed. [SBL LXX and Cognate Studies, 1973] Vol. 4, pp. 113–114). Charles says Josephus was aware of these claims and against them he reacts (Vol. 2, p. 409). If this were the view of Moses' end that Josephus knew, however, his response is meaningless. To say that Moses died would not protect against such a double vision of his end. That Moses died and was buried would counter only a bodily assumption into heaven.

54. This explains the claim of Celsus that Moses attained to divine honors (Origen, *Against Celsus* 1:21).

55. Since miraculous birth traditions could belong to the tradition of a divine man as well as to the mythology of immortals, reference to the supernatural conception of Moses does not in and of itself establish belief in Moses as an immortal. Cf. David Daube, *The New Testament and Rabbinic Judaism* (London: Athlone, 1956), pp. 5–7; W. D. Davies, *The Setting of the Sermon on the Mount* (Cambridge: Cambridge University Press, 1964), pp. 81–82; for the supernatural conception of Moses in the Passover Haggadah. The reference to Moses' beauty in Josephus (*Ant.* 2.9,5§224) points to his use of a *theios anēr* tradition of Moses' birth (*Contra* Davies, *Setting*, p. 82).

56. Eventually reduced to ridiculous extremes, the mythology of immortals was even applied to the relatives of emperors, e.g., Julia Drusilla, sister of Caligula. (Seneca, *Pumpkinification of Claudius* 1.)

57. Cf. E. I. McQueen, "Quintus Curtius Rufus," in *Latin Biography*, T. A. Dorey, ed. (London: Routledge & Kegan Paul, 1967), p. 20.

58. Arrian, *Anabasis Alexandri* 7:27.

59. *Ibid.*, 7:30. This may very well mean that Arrian was willing

to regard Alexander as a divine man but not as an immortal (see below).

60. *Alexander Romance* 3:30. That is, Alexander asks to join the Olympians as Hercules and Dionysus did.

61. A quite different treatment of Alexander's divinity can be found in Quintus Curtius Rufus, 10:10:9–13.

62. Dio Cassius, 45:1.

63. *Ibid.*, 56:46.

64. Even when Augustus is not spoken of in "birth/ascension" mythology, he is idealized to the extreme. Cf., e.g., Nicolaus of Damascus' *Life of Augustus* where Augustus is flawless.

65. Suetonius, *Lives of the Caesars*, "Augustus," 94:4.

66. *Ibid.*

67. Diogenes Laertius, *Lives* 8:68.

68. *Ibid.*, 8:69, 70.

69. Philostratus, *Life of Apollonius of Tyana* 1:4.

70. *Ibid.*, 1:6.

71. *Ibid.*, 8:30.

72. *Ibid.*, 8:31.

73. On the founders of cities as objects of religious devotion, cf. Pausanias, 10:4:10. Cf. also C. B. Wells, "The Hellenistic Orient," in *The Idea of History in the Ancient Near East*, R. C. Dentan, ed. (New Haven: Yale University Press, 1955) p. 157.

74. Seneca, *The Pumpkinification of Claudius* 1.

75. *Ibid.*, 9.

76. Lucian, *The Parliament of the Gods*, esp. 7–10, 14. Cf. a similar point in Cicero, *Tusculan Disputations* 1:12; *Recognitions of Clement* 10:24–25; *Clementine Homilies* 6:22.

77. Lucian, *The Passing of Peregrinus* 39. The reference to Olympus indicates that Peregrinus was yet another mortal accepted by the Olympians.

78. *Ibid.*, 40.

79. The miraculous birth traditions, when present, speak of the specialness of the demigod during his lifetime. At the same time, he remains mortal.

80. This is not the same thing one finds in Judaism in the ascensions of Enoch and Elijah. These men are taken up to heaven, but they do not become deities. (a) The closest Elijah comes to being treated as an immortal is in the *Acts of Pilate* 15:1. There is a reference to 2 Kings

2:16–18 but the reading is distinct: "And they persuaded Elisha and he went with them. And they searched for him three days and did not find him, and they knew that he had been taken up." (*New Testament Apocrypha* W. Schneemelcher, ed. [Philadelphia: Westminster, 1963] Vol. 1, p. 464). So in the *Acts of Pilate* the Jews search for Jesus and do not find him, the implication being that he has been taken up. Still, Elijah does not join the gods. (b) The closest Enoch comes to being treated as an immortal is in *2 Enoch*: his ascent to heaven is in the company of the angel (36:2) or angels (55:1) of God; he is taken up amidst darkness, so that those standing and talking with him do not understand what has happened until they receive a heavenly message (67:1–3); when they understand that Enoch has been taken up, the people erect an altar and offer sacrifice "before the Lord's face" (68:5–7). Though the debt to the mythology of immortals is undeniable, Enoch still remains a man and does not become a god.

81. Hans Dieter Betz, *Lukian von Samosata und das Neue Testament* (Berlin: Akademie, 1961) seems unaware of the distinction. He treats the two concepts as though they were one. Cf. also his "Jesus as Divine Man," in *Jesus and the Historian*, F. T. Trotter, ed. (Philadelphia: Westminster, 1968) and H. J. Rose, "Herakles and the Gospels," *HTR* 31 (1938), 126.

82. Josephus, *Antiquities* 3.7,7§180. Josephus also speaks of (1) Solomon as having a godlike understanding (ὡς θείαν ἔχοντι διάνοιαν) (*Ant.* 8.2,1§34), (2) Isaiah as θεῖος (*Ant.* 20.2,1§35), (3) Daniel as esteemed for his divine power (θειότητος) (*Ant.* 10.10,5§268).

83. Philo, *On the Virtues* 177; *Life of Moses* 1. 158. In his *Embassy to Gaius* 77–114, is found one of the clearest statements in antiquity of the typology, eternals/immortals.

84. Plato, e.g., is a divine man born of a woman and Apollo in Plutarch, *Symposiacs* 8:1:2, and Laertius, *Lives* 3:45.

85. Cicero, *Tusculan Disputations* 1:14; Plutarch, "Pelopidas" 16; Dio Chrysostom, *Discourse* 31:16.

86. Diodorus, *Library of History* 6:1.

87. *Ibid.*, 1:13.

88. Dio Chrysostom, *Discourse* 2:78; 69:1.

89. Pseudo-Lucian, *Cynic* 13, says of Theseus that he was the best man of his day.

90. Tiede, *Charismatic Figure*.

91. F. C. Conybeare, Loeb Classical Library, Vol. 1, p. viii.

92. Cf. Howard Clark Kee, "Aretalogy and Gospel," *JBL* 92 (1973), 410.

93. Philostratus, *Life of Apollonius* 1:1–2; Cf. also 8:7:[4].

94. This is not the same distinction as that of Cleanthes who believed that there were two Hercules, one a god, the other a hero. Cf. W. L. Knox, "The Divine Hero Christology in the New Testament," *HTR* 41 (1948), 235, n.14.

95. Justin Martyr, *1 Apology* 21.

96. *Ibid., Dialogue with Trypho* 69. Theophilus of Antioch, *To Autolycus* 1:13, uses the same technique. He says of those who deride the Christians' belief in the resurrection: " . . . you actually believe that Herakles, who burned himself up, is alive and that Asclepius, struck by lightning, was raised (ἐγηγέρθει)."

97. *Dialogue* 69, 70; *1 Apology* 54.

98. *1 Apology* 58.

99. *Dialogue* 69; also 52–54; *1 Apology* 54.

100. *Dialogue* 69.

101. Reginald H. Fuller, *The Foundations of New Testament Christology* (New York: Scribner's, 1965) pp. 184–97. For our purposes it is not necessary to resolve the debate over whether Hellenistic Jewish Christianity is an appropriate designation for the circles from which exaltation Christology came. Cf. I. H. Marshall, "Palestinian and Hellenistic Christianity: Some Critical Comments," *NTS* 19 (1973), 271–88.

102. According to Ferdinand Hahn, *The Titles of Jesus in Christology* (London: Lutterworth, 1969) pp. 289–90, Hellenistic Judaism took the specifically pagan edge off the *theios anēr* concept by seeing miracles as due to the Spirit, and by averting all thought of deification.

103. W. L. Knox, *HTR* 41 (1948), 229–30, rightly thinks Rom. 1:3–4 reflects such a pattern.

104. The pagan way of thinking did not necessarily involve moral grossness. Plutarch, *Numa*, 4 and *Symposiacs*, 8:1:3, followed the Egyptians in thinking that one must not suppose the act was accomplished through the god in person having intercourse with a mortal woman. The act was accomplished through the agency of a "spirit of god" (*pneuma theou*).

105. "Romulus," 28:2–3; cf. also Cicero, *The Republic* 1:41, citing Ennius. Phil. 2:6–11, among the christological hymns, may reflect this pattern.

106. Reginald H. Fuller, *Foundations*, pp. 197, 248, is incorrect when he claims that Hellenistic Jewish Christianity had not yet raised the ontic question of the divinity of the exalted. A supernatural conception would be interpreted ontically in Mediterranean antiquity. This is the significance of the term *demigods* (ἡμιθέοις); they are half gods (cf. Luke 1:35). Further, the Christian resurrection/exaltation tradition would convey ontic change. The tradition in Rom. 6:9 states precisely what was understood to have happened to the immortals (cf. Philo, *Life of Moses* 2.288; Plutarch, "Romulus," 28:6–8). Against Fuller, it seems that the mythology of immortals offered one way for some early Christians to deal with the ontic problem of their simultaneous belief in one God and in Jesus as Lord. The one God was conceived as *the* eternal; Jesus as *the* immortal.

107. The presence of the two heavenly figures at Jesus' ascent in Acts 1:9–11 and in the *Gospel of Peter* 9:34–10:42 is similar to the descent of Hercules and Dionysus to take Alexander back to heaven with them (cf. Pseudo-Callisthenes, *Alexander Romance*).

108. Elias Bickerman, "Das leere Grab," *ZNW* 23 (1924), 281–92; N. Q. Hamilton, "Resurrection Tradition and the Composition of Mark," *JBL* 84 (1965), 415–21; T. J. Weeden, *Mark—Traditions in Conflict* (Philadelphia: Fortress, 1971), pp. 106–108, have all argued that the empty tomb story is a translation narrative. If the empty tomb story was a translation tale, then we may ask whether Paul's omission of reference to the empty tomb might be linked with his preference for another christological pattern.

109. A. Ehrhardt, "The Disciples of Emmaus," *NTS* 10 (1963/64), 187–201, regards Luke 24:13–35 as similar to the Romulus tradition (e.g., Dionysus of Halicarnassus, 2:63:3). This is reinforced by the fact that Plutarch's description of Romulus' appearance ("Romulus," 28) conforms in essentials to the form of resurrection appearances elaborated by C. H. Dodd, "The Appearances of the Risen Christ," in *Studies in the Gospels*, D. E. Nineham, ed. (Oxford: Blackwell, 1955), pp. 9–36.

110. Cf. Charles H. Talbert, *Literary Patterns, Theological Themes, and the Genre of Luke-Acts* (Missoula, Montana: Scholars Press, 1974), Ch. 6.

111. So, most recently, R. H. Stein, "A Short Note on Mark 14:28 and 16:7," *NTS* 20 (1974), 445–52.

112. Arnaldo Momigliano, *The Development of Greek Biography* (Cambridge, Mass.: Harvard University Press, 1971), p. 9.

3
Mythical Structure—2

According to Bultmann, in order to claim that the canonical gospels belong to any ancient genre it would be necessary, among other things, to show that in this genre the outer form or structure was determined by myth. In the previous chapter we demonstrated that the same myth of immortals which controlled the accounts of a number of pagan and Jewish sources, at least some of which were prior to the time of the writing of the Christian gospels, also ordered the synoptic gospels. In this chapter we turn to the myth which controls the Jesus material in the Fourth Gospel. Our aim is twofold. First, to describe the myth and its impact on early Christianity, especially in the Gospel of John. Second, to explain why no Graeco-Roman biographies employ it and to explore the implications of this fact for our genre discussions.

The Descending-Ascending Redeemer in the Milieu of Early Christianity

In spite of its popularity, the contention that the Christian conception of Jesus as a descending-ascending savior figure was derived from the gnostic redeemer myth faces serious problems.[1] Three are widely noted; another needs attention. (1) The sources from which our knowledge of the gnostic myth comes are late:[2] e.g., the Naassene hymn, the hymn of the Pearl, the Mandean materials, the Manichean evidence, the accounts in the church fathers, and the Nag Hammadi documents. Sources from Chenoboskion such as the *Paraphrase of Shem*,[3] the *Apocalypse of Adam*,[4] and the *Second Treatise of the Great Seth*[5] do contain a myth of a redeemer that is only superficially Christianized. The gnostics thus may not have derived their myth from Christians, but it does not follow either that Christians got it from gnostics or that it is pre-Christian.[6]   (2) A redeemer myth is not essential to gnosticism.[7] Though gnosticism may contain a redeemer myth (e.g., the Naassene hymn), it may exist without one.   In Carpocrates' system, for example, Jesus' soul remembered what it had seen in its circuit with the unbegotten god.[8]   The Ophites in Origen's *Against Celsus* know of no descending-ascending redeemer.   They look to an earthly being who fetches gnosis from heaven.[9]   In *Poimandres* the prophet is the recipient of a vision in rapture.   He then teaches the way of salvation.   Indeed, the proto-gnosticism of Paul's opponents in 1 Corinthians apparently did not contain a redeemer myth.[10] Such evidence demands that a distinction be drawn between two issues: whether or not there was a pre-Christian gnostic redeemer myth, and whether or not there was a pre-Christian gnosticism. Since a redeemer myth is not constitutive for gnosticism, the existence of a pre-Christian gnosis is no guarantee for the presence of a gnostic redeemer myth.[11]   (3) In the Christian sources where the gnostic myth has often been assumed to be influential (e.g., the Fourth Gospel), there is no ontological identity between Christ and the believers as in gnosticism.   There is, in the Christian writings, no preexistence of the soul or redeemed redeemer.[12]   Given these difficulties, why the attractiveness of the gnostic hypothesis?

The pattern of descent-ascent in the gnostic redeemer myth "has been and remains the strongest support for the hypothesis" that early Christian Christology is connected with gnostic mythology.[13] (4) Generally overlooked is the fact that myths of descending-ascending redeemers are found elsewhere in the Mediterranean world prior to and parallel with the origins of Christianity.   If so, then the strongest support for the gnostic hypothesis collapses and the question deserves reexamination.

The Graeco-Roman mythology is not as well known to New Testament scholars as that of gnosticism but it is instructive nonetheless.   For example, in his *Metamorphoses* (7 C.E.) Ovid tells of the visit of Jupiter and Mercury in the guise of mortals, seeking a place for rest and finding it only in the humble home of old Baucis and Philemon.   The gods save the couple from the destruction of

the neighborhood by water and grant them not only their prayer
that they would not be separated by death but also a type of immortality by changing them into intertwining trees near the god's
temple.[14]   Acts 14:8–18 shows that this myth of descending-
ascending gods was known to Christians in the first century.
Tacitus, in his *Histories* (published in the reign of Trajan, 98–117
C.E.), tells of the origin of the Serapis cult in Ptolemaic times. A
young man of more than human size appeared to Soter and in-
structed him to send to Pontus and fetch his statue. The god told
Ptolemy that if he did as he was directed, it "would bring prosperity
to the realm" and the city would be "great and illustrious." Serapis then ascended to heaven in a blaze of fire.[15]

   The descent-ascent mythology could be used by Graeco-Roman
authors to interpret the lives of historical figures just as gnostics
employed their myth for Simon, Menander, and Christ. Vergil's
Fourth Eclogue runs:

> The last age of the Sibyl's poem is now come. . . . Now a new
> offspring is *sent down from high heaven.* Do thou, chaste Lucina,
> favor the birth of the child under whom the iron breed will first
> cease and a golden race arise throughout the world. Now shall
> *thine own Apollo bear sway.* (Italics added)

Augustus' birth is here viewed in terms of the myth of Apollo's
descent for redemptive purposes (i.e., cessation of war and estab-
lishment of peace). Horace's *Odes* I:ii (23 B.C.E.) reflects a similar tendency. The odist asks: "Whom of the gods shall the folk
call to the needs of the falling empire?" (25–26); "To whom shall
Jupiter assign the task of atoning for our guilt?" (29–30); then
various gods are addressed, Apollo, Mars, and finally Mercury. It
is the last of these whose descent is described as a change of form,
the assumption on earth of the guise of man (41–44); it is the
epiphany of Mercury that is used to interpret the career of Augustus. The petition closes, "Late mayest thou return to the skies and
long mayest thou be pleased to dwell amid Quirinus' folk" (45–
46). From these few examples, we see that a Graeco-Roman
mythology of descending-ascending gods who appear on earth for
redemptive purposes both existed early enough to be available for

Christian appropriation and had, by the beginning of our era, already been used to interpret the lives of historical figures.

The Hellenistic-Jewish mythology of a descending-ascending redeemer is usually overlooked or denied. Thomas Fawcett is representative when he says pre-Christian Judaism did not have any one myth which would account for the primitive Christian concept of Jesus' descent from heaven.[16] Since Jewish mythology has received inadequate attention, this chapter will focus on it. We will first attempt to establish the existence of a *katabasis-anabasis* pattern for redemption figures in ancient Judaism and second, argue that this Jewish myth, in various forms, served as the source for certain early Christian speech about Jesus.[17]

The descent-ascent pattern is connected with redemption figures in at least two streams of ancient Judaism. On the one hand, the wisdom tradition reflects such a myth. In contrast to Proverbs 8:22–36 where heavenly wisdom is accessible to the man who earnestly seeks it, certain writings near the beginning of our era speak of the *descent* of wisdom from the heavens with saving intent. In Sirach 24 preexistent wisdom comes down from heaven, appears on earth among men, tabernacling in Jacob as the law. Baruch 3:27–4:4 is similar, heavenly wisdom being given by God to Israel. She appears on earth and lives among the people as the law. In these two sources the wisdom myth is used to interpret the meaning of an historical entity, the law.[18] The Wisdom of Solomon refers to preexistent wisdom's being sent from the heavens (9:10) as a savior figure both in this world (7:27; 8:10) and for the next (6:18–20; 8:13, 17), the author actually speaking of being "saved by wisdom" (9:18; cf. 10:1, 4, 6, 13, 15, etc.).[19] Both 2 Esdras 5:9–10 and 2 Baruch 48:36 refer to the *ascent* of wisdom, departing the earth during the crisis preceding the end. 1 Enoch 42:1–2 contains a reference both to the *descent* and the *ascent* of wisdom. She comes down from heaven but, finding no dwelling place, returns to heaven and takes her seat among the angels.[20]

How does one explain the difference of these sources from Proverbs 8 and their similarity with one another? The usual explanation has been the hypothesis of a common myth used by all (whether from gnosticism[21] or from the Isis cult[22]). It may just as easily be explained by the changed theological climate for understanding wisdom in Judaism,[23] a change paralleled by Greek developments described in the latter parts of Gilbert Murray's *Five Stages of Greek Religion*.[24]   However one explains the phenomena, the "hypostasized Wisdom of late Jewish literature . . . is an anonymous heavenly redeemer figure."[25]   Its pattern (*katabasis-anabasis*), function (soteriological), and use to interpret an historical entity (the law), show the wisdom myth near the beginning of our era to be analogous to gnostic, Graeco-Roman, and Christian ones.

However, Jewish angelology also employs the *katabasis-anabasis* pattern for redemption figures.[26]   This is true both for the *mal'ach* Yahweh and for the archangels.   Consider first the angel of the Lord.[27]   (1) The Jewish scriptures in both their Hebrew and Greek forms speak of the *mal'ach* Yahweh who is sometimes indistinguishable from God himself.[28]   So one finds the paradoxical juxtaposition of two conceptions: the angel is sent by God (e.g., Gen. 19:1,13) and, the angel is God in action (e.g., Gen. 22:11–18).   Hence the angel is closely identified with God's name (e.g., Gen. 16:13a; Exod. 23:20–21).   (2) The *mal'ach* appears sometimes as a man or men.   For example, in Genesis 18:2, 22 we hear of three men who ate with Abraham (v. 8).   Philo (*Abraham* 22, 113) says, "though they neither ate nor drank, they gave the appearance of both eating and drinking."   Philo confirms what the text (vv. 10, 13, 17, 20) affirms: the men represent the *mal'ach* (cf. Josephus, *Ant.* 1:11:2 §197).   Genesis 32:24, 25 speaks of a man, though Hosea 12:5 says it was the *mal'ach*.   Judges 13:6, 8 calls the angel a man of God, but v. 16 makes it clear that he will not eat food.   (3) The angel's coming and going are sometimes explicitly spoken of as a descent and an ascent.   For example, Exodus 3:8 has the Lord or the *mal'ach* (v. 2) say, "I have come down,"[29] and Judges 13:20 states the "angel ascended."   (4) Among the functions of the angel are redemptive activities.   In Genesis 19:12ff. he saves Lot; in Genesis 22:11ff. he saves Isaac; in Genesis 48:15–16 he is the angel "who redeemed me from all evil"; in Exodus 3:2ff. he comes down to deliver the people from the hand of the Egyptians;[30] in Judges 6:11ff. he came down to send Gideon to deliver the people. If the "angel of his presence" in Isaiah 63:9 is the *mal'ach*, then he is the one who "saved them, in his love and pity he redeemed them...."[31]

We now turn to the archangels.[32] In Tobit (second century B.C.E.) Raphael is sent to heal both Tobit and Sarah, the daughter of Raguel (3:16–17). Raphael accompanies Tobias on his journey, keeps him safe and sound (5:21) and gives Tobias both the remedy for his father's eye ailment and a means of ridding his bride of the demon. As a result Tobias drives the demon away (8:3) and cures his father's blindness (11:8, 12–14, 16). Reciting Raphael's benefits, Tobias says to his father:

> He has led me back to you safely,
> he cured my wife,
> he obtained the money for me,
> and he also healed you (12:3).

The angel then says to father and son:

> God *sent me* to heal you and your daughter-in-law Sarah. I am Raphael, one of the seven holy angels ... (12:14–15a). All those days I merely appeared to you and did not eat or drink, but you were seeing a vision. And now give thanks to God, for *I am ascending to him who sent me* (12:19–20a). (Italics added)

Here in a this-worldly context we meet an angelic redemption figure who descends and ascends and who, while on earth, appears to be a man.

In the Hellenistic-Jewish *Joseph and Asenath* (first century B.C.E.)[33] Asenath is held up as the model proselyte. Her passage from idolatry is facilitated by an angel, the Prince of the heavenly hosts. Following Asenath's prayer there was a cleft in the heavens and a man, flashing with light, stood over her (14). The archangel said:

> God has heard your prayer. He has looked upon your sorrow and tears, and has forgiven your sin. Be of good cheer, for your name is written in the Book of Life ... From this day forth you shall eat the bread of life and drink the cup of immortality, and be anointed

with the oil of joy. . . . many shall in like manner come to Him
through your example by repentance (15).

Asenath then wants to feed the angel. He sends her for a honey-
comb which is miraculously there, eats of it himself, and gives some
to the maiden, saying, "Now you have received the food of life and
your youth shall know no old age and your beauty shall never
fade." In this context he also says, "You are blessed, Asenath, for
you have seen some of the secret things of God; it is of this honey-
comb that the angels eat in Paradise . . . and whoever tastes it shall
not die forever" (16). Then, after blessing her seven maidens
(17), he goes back to heaven, with Asenath recognizing his true
identity. Here we find the descent and ascent of an archangel, who
appears to Asenath as a man, connected with her redemption from
pagan idolatry and her gaining of immortality.

The *Testament of Job* (early first century C.E.)[34] which probably comes from Egyptian Judaism presents us with a descending-
ascending angelic redeemer.[35] Chapters 2–5 tell the story of
Job's conversion. Job is at a loss to know whether the god worshiped in the nearby temple is the one who made the heaven and
earth. His conversion results from a night vision in which the
angel comes to him as a voice in a great light for the purpose of the
salvation of his soul (3:5b [5]). He tells Job all that the Lord
commanded (4:2), including the promise of the restoration of
goods lost in this life because of Satan and an ultimate resurrection
from the dead if Job endures (4:6–8). After sealing Job, the
angel departs (5:2). By this revelation Job is set apart from the
rest of deceived mankind. Chapters 2–27 show him overcoming
Satan by the endurance based on the knowledge of the future hope,
the heavenly city, imparted to him by the angel.[36] Once again,
this time in an early first-century Hellenistic-Jewish source, we find
a descending-ascending angelic redeemer figure.

The Hellenistic-Jewish *Apocalypse of Moses* (beginning of the
first century C.E.[37]) describes Adam's death in terms of angelic
descent and ascent. When Adam dies, the angels descend and take
his soul into heaven, interceding for him before God (33:1–5).
Adam is pardoned by God and washed in the lake of heaven by one

of the seraphim (37:2–3). Then the archangel Michael takes
Adam's soul into Paradise in the third heaven to await the last day
(37:4–6). There is no doubt that in this document the descent
and ascent of the angelic hosts is for the sake of the redemption of
Adam. Such joint redemptive activity of angels, seraphim, and
archangel perhaps prompted rabbinic protests like that of (a)
j.*Berakot* 9:1: "If trouble comes to a man, he must not invoke
either Michael or Gabriel but God, who will hear him";[38] or, (b)
the refrain, "I—not by means of an angel and not by means of a
messenger," which is found in Sifre Deuteronomy 42 and 325, the
Mekilta on Exodus 12:12, in Version B of *Aboth de Rabbi Nathan*
where it is said that Moses received the law not from the mouth of
an angel and not from the mouth of a seraph, and in the Passover
Haggadah where it is said that the Lord brought the people forth
out of Egypt "not by means of an angel, and not by means of a
seraph, and not by means of a messenger."[39] These protests by
rabbinic Judaism confirm the fact that in some circles of ancient
Jewish piety people looked to angels, archangels, and seraphim as
redeemer figures.

The *Testament of Abraham* (first century C.E.)[40] describes the
descents and ascents of the archangel Michael, the purpose of
whose coming to Abraham is twofold. On the one hand, the
archangel "told him everything which he had heard from the Most
High" (9:17–18) which included the announcement of his death.
On the other hand, he gave Abraham the assurance that he would
go to his Master among the good (1:5–10). Hence he tries to get
the patriarch "to follow him" into heaven (7:4; 8:11; 15:28–29;
19:8; 20:21). Isaac describes his dream about the deaths of his
father and mother in this way:

> I saw the heaven opened and I saw a luminous man *descending*
> from heaven, shining more than seven suns. And this man of the
> sunlight form came and took the sun from my head and *went
> back up into the heavens* from which he had descended. . . . And
> after a little time . . . I saw this man coming forth from heaven
> a second time, and he took the moon from me, from my head. I
> wept greatly and entreated that luminous man and said, "My lord,

take not my glory from me. . . ." He said, "Allow them to be taken up to the king on high, for he wants them there" (7:3–17).[41]

(Italics added)

In this source we meet an archangel described as a man who descends and ascends. The purpose of his coming and going is to take Abraham and Sarah, Isaac's parents, to God, an activity that is certainly redemptive.

Origen uses the *Prayer of Joseph* (first or second century C.E.)[42] to add weight to his argument that John the Baptist was an angel who assumed a body for the sake of bearing witness to Christ. This apocryphal work current among the Hebrews, he says, spoke of Jacob-Israel as the archangel of God, the chief captain among the sons of God, a ruling spirit, the firstborn of every creature, who descended to earth and tabernacled among men.[43] He fought with the angel Uriel when the latter tried to exalt himself beyond his rightful position. Once again, we find the typical pattern of angelic descent (with ascent implied), involving again taking bodily form and successfully struggling with evil. The conclusion seems irresistible: in certain circles of ancient Jewish angelology, both B.C.E. and in the first and second centuries C.E., there existed a mythology with a descent-ascent pattern, in which the redeemer figure descends, takes human form, and then ascends back to heaven either after or in connection with his saving activity.[44]

Though the *mal'ach* Yahweh and archangel traditions were originally distinct, by the beginning of our era they had, in certain circles at least,[45] merged into one. Either one of the archangels could absorb the functions of the others so that he was almost the equivalent of the ancient *mal'ach*[46] or the scriptural references to the angel of the Lord could refer to an archangel.[47] Whether separately or in synthetic form, the two Jewish traditions of angelology provided a myth of a descending-ascending redeemer figure alongside a similar mythology in Jewish wisdom literature.

In some Jewish circles the angel and wisdom traditions merged not only with one another but also with the concepts of the logos and the firstborn son, among others. The identification of wisdom and angel is made already in 1 Enoch 42:1–2 where it is said that when heavenly wisdom came down, found no dwelling place, and returned to heaven, she took her seat among the angels.[48] The same identification is found in the Wisdom of Solomon in 10:6 where wisdom is identified, both with the *mal'ach* who delivered Lot, and in the parallelism between 10:15–16, where wisdom delivers Israel from Egypt amidst wonders and signs, and 15:15, where the *mal'ach* Yahweh performs the same task. The merger of concepts and traditions in the Wisdom of Solomon, however, goes further than the mere equation of wisdom and angel. In 9:1–2 wisdom and logos are equated;[49] in 9:17 the parallelism seems to link wisdom and Holy Spirit, while in 18:15 logos and angel are identified. The resulting configuration yields a divine redeemer figure who is variously identified as wisdom—logos—angel—Holy Spirit.

Philo offers further evidence for the merger of traditions and concepts. Though on occasion he represents either the logos as derived from wisdom (*On Dreams* 1.108f.) or Sophia as derivative from the logos (*On Flight and Finding* 97), in *Allegorical Interpretation* 1.65 he makes the two completely identical: ἡ [σοφία] δέ ἐστιν ὁ θεοῦ λόγος.[50] He can identify pneuma with wisdom (e.g., *On the Creation* 135; *On the Giants* 22, 27). He can equate the logos and angel, either archangel (*Who Is the Heir?* 42, 205) or *mal'ach* (e.g., *On the Cherubim* 35; *Questions and Answers on Exodus* 2:13). He sometimes links the Word, the firstborn Son, and the angel of Yahweh (*On Husbandry* 51). At other times the Son, the logos, and the archangel are meshed.[51] For example, in *Confusion of Tongues* Philo says:

> But if there be any as yet unfit to be called a son of God, let him press to take his place under God's First-born, the Word, who holds the eldership among the angels, their ruler (ἀρχάγγελον) as it were. And many other names are his, for he is called, "the Beginning," and the Name of God, and His Word, and the Man after His Image, and "he that sees," that is Israel. . . . For if we have not yet become fit to be thought sons of God yet we may be sons of His invisible image, the most holy Word. For the Word is the eldest-born image of God.[52]

Yet another designation for the many-named Logos or Wisdom is
high priest (e.g., *On Dreams* 1.215; *On Flight and Finding* 108).
In Philo, therefore, we meet a heavenly, divine figure,[53] Son—
Word—Angel—Wisdom—High Priest—Man, the many named
one.[54] Here we can see clearly the merger of wisdom and angel
traditions, with others also brought into the synthesis.

Two objections are usually raised at this point: the logos figure
in Philo is not personal and, Philo's logos is not a redeemer. On
the one hand, it is asserted that although Philo sometimes speaks of
this heavenly figure in personal terms (e.g., Son, Man, Angel, High
Priest), for him the logos is never truly personal. It is the Platonic
world of ideas conceived of as expressing the mind of God.[55] As
such it is the medium by which the world approaches God.[56] On
the other hand, it is contended that the logos in Philo has only
cosmological and psychological, not soteriological functions.[57]

Neither of these objections poses a serious obstacle for our thesis. The first may be countered with three observations: the
mythology of a heavenly, divine redeemer figure alternately described as Logos—Wisdom—Angel—Spirit existed in Alexandrian
Judaism prior to Philo (e.g., Wisdom of Solomon), and in this
mythology the redeemer figure was personal;[58] Philo's writings
assume this myth and set about to interpret it; his allegorical reading of the myth does take it to be the impersonal philosophical
entity scholars claim. For our purposes it is sufficient to note that
whereas Philo's own personal stance is a demythologized one, the
materials he is reinterpreting give us an indirect witness to the
existence of the myth in the Jewish community of his time.[59]
While it is, therefore, correct to say that for Philo the logos is not
personal, it is also accurate to note that he is allegorizing a myth of
a personal being with many names.[60]

The second objection is cancelled by the following three facts:
(a) the basic orientation of Philo's exegesis is soteriological. He is
concerned with the question of how man can know God; (b) the
logos with many names is, in Philo, a "mediating figure which
comes forth from God and establishes a link between the remotely
transcendent God and the world or man, and yet which also repre-

sents man to God as a high priest (*On the Giants* 52) and advo-
cate" (*Life of Moses* 2.133; *On One Who Is Heir* 42).[62] That is,
this figure is both revealer and intercessor. This, in Philo's context,
is definitely soteriological; (c) though Philo's allegorical interpretation does not treat the many-named logos as a personal redeemer,
the myth on which he is working most definitely does (e.g., *Wisdom
of Solomon*). Again, Philo is an indirect witness to the myth of a
heavenly, divine redeemer figure in Egyptian Judaism, a myth in
which wisdom and angel streams of thought had merged and drawn
into their orbit other concepts such as Son of God, Word of God,
Man in God's image, and High Priest.

Still further evidence for this view comes from a collection of
fragments contained in the *Apostolic Constitutions*, published in
1915 by Bousset who believed they reflected Jewish liturgy.[63]
E. R. Goodenough accepted Bousset's thesis and regarded the fragments as reflecting the same type of syncretistic Judaism as that
found in Philo.[64] Though they cannot be dated with any certainty
prior to the second century C.E., they confirm the existence of an
ongoing Jewish tradition in which the wisdom and angel conceptions have merged with one another and with others such as Son,
Word, and High Priest. Fragment 7 (*Constitutions* 8:12:6–27) is
especially clear about the many-named heavenly, divine figure. In
7:7 we hear that God has begotten his only Son before all ages, that
is, God the Logos, the living Sophia, the firstborn of every creature,
the angel of the Great Counsel, God's High Priest. Goodenough
proposed, further, that three more fragments besides those of Bousset be considered Jewish in origin.[65] If the first (Fragment 14,
Constitutions 7:26:1–3) is accepted, then the Son who created the
world (cf. Fragment 7) is also the one through whom men gain
knowledge and immortality. The many-named one is a redeemer.

This syncretistic practice of Hellenistic Judaism is a part of the
tendency of the larger culture of the time to think in terms of one
heavenly reality which could be addressed or described by many
names. Cleanthes' *Hymn to Zeus* begins: "Thou, O Zeus, are
praised above all gods: Many are thy names and thine is all power
for ever." A third-century B.C.E. inscription by Artemidorus of

Perga who settled on the island of Thera speaks of "this Hecate, of many names."[66] Plutarch makes the same point in his *On Isis and Osiris*, especially 67, 70, 78. The one logos which orders all things is given different modes of address among different peoples. Tacitus, *History* 4:84, says the god Serapis was identified by some as Asclepius, by others as Osiris, by still others as Jupiter, but by most as Pluto. Diogenes Laertius says that the Stoics hold that "God is one and the same with Reason, Fate, and Zeus; he is also called by many other names."[67] No passage is clearer than that in Apuleius' *Metamorphoses* where Lucius cries out to Isis:

> O blessed queen of heaven, whether thou be the Dame Ceres . . .
> or the celestial Venus . . . or . . . the sister of the god Phoebus . . .
> or . . . Proserpine. . . . by whatsoever name or fashion or shape
> it is lawful to call upon Thee, I pray Thee. . . .

Lucius' cry to the goddess is heard. Isis replies:

> For the Phrygians . . . call me the Mother of the gods at Pessinus;
> the Athenians . . . Cecropian Minerva; the Cyprians . . . Paphian
> Venus; the Cretans . . . Dietynnian Diana; the Sicilians . . . infernal
> Proserpine; the Eleusinians . . . Ceres; some Juno, others Bellona,
> others Hecate, others Rhamnusia . . . and the Egyptians . . . do
> call me by my true name, Queen Isis.[68]

It is inevitable that some Jews, living in this type of world, would conceive of one heavenly redeemer figure who descended and ascended with a redemptive function and who could be addressed or spoken of with many names, for example, Word, Wisdom, Angel, Son, Man, High Priest. At the same time, it is also true that other Jews continued to maintain the traditions separately (e.g., either angel or wisdom) or in varying stages of merger (e.g., wisdom—word merged, but separate from angel, as in Sirach; or angel—son—spirit merged, as in the *Prayer of Joseph*, but separate from logos and wisdom). The conclusion is irresistible. A myth of a heavenly redeemer who descended and ascended in the course of his/her saving work existed in pre-Christian Judaism and alongside first- and second-century Christianity. It existed in a multiplicity of forms, with the different varieties depending on the degree of syncretism existing at a given time and place. In its extreme form, the diverse traditions had run together so that the communities conceived of one redeemer who was many-named. Hellenistic Judaism, just as Graeco-Roman paganism, gnosticism, and early Christianity, employed mythologies of descending-ascending re- deemers near the beginning of our era. Having established this fact, it is now necessary to ask about the relationship between the Jewish myths and that of the Christians.

Early Christian Use of the Jewish
Katabasis-Anabasis Mythology

We must now explore the possible use of certain forms of the Jewish redeemer mythology by six selected noncanonical Christian authors and by three New Testament writers. Since Jewish and pagan mythology employed, from pre-Christian times, a *pattern* (descent-ascent) and a *function* (soteriological) analogous to that of the Christian myth of the redeemer, either could conceivably have been the source of the Christian usage. In order to determine which of these, if either, constituted the source for the Christian mythology, *terminology* must be decisive. What we will be looking for are signs of a descent-ascent pattern, used in connection with the church's savior figure, in connection with a cluster of names, titles, or other linguistic characteristics of the Jewish myths in their various forms. We begin with an examination of six selected non- canonical writings.

Justin Martyr presents us with as full a Christian adaptation of the Jewish synthesis as can be found in the second century. Though Justin's Christology has usually been regarded as an appropriation of Stoic logos thought (e.g., 1 *Apol.* 46; 2 *Apol.* 10), sometimes, especially in the *Dialogue with Trypho*, we find Christ spoken of in terms of the Son-Wisdom-Word-Angel vocabulary of Hellenistic Judaism. This terminology is used for his descent-ascent Christol- ogy (*Trypho* 38, 48, 56, 59, 61, 126, 128). This descending- ascending many-named one functions in Justin as a savior or re- vealer of God to man (e.g., 56, 128). Since the pattern, function, and terminology of Justin's Christology in the *Dialogue* corresponds to the mythology of Hellenistic Judaism, it is difficult to resist the conclusion that this Christian is using the Jewish categories.

In *Dialogue* 61, for example, Justin says:

> God has begotten of Himself a certain rational Power as a Beginning before all other creatures. The Holy Spirit indicates this Power by varying titles, sometimes . . . *Son*, or *Wisdom*, or *Angel*, or . . . *Word*. He even called Himself Commander-in-Chief when He appeared in human guise to Joshua, the son of Nun. Indeed, He can justly lay claim to all these titles from the fact both that He performs the Father's will and that He was begotten by an act of the Father's will.[69]   (Italics added)

The same cluster of Son-Angel-Word-Wisdom titles occurs again in *Dialogue* 128–129. Elsewhere we find combinations of Son— Wisdom—Angel (*Dial.* 62; 126); Son—Word—Angel (1 *Apol.* 63); or Son—Angel—Priest—Man (*Dial.* 34). When Justin refers to Christ as Angel, sometimes it is to the *mal'ach* (e.g., *Dial.* 56, 61–62, 59, 60, 128), sometimes to the *mal'ach* bearing the name Israel (e.g., *Dial.* 75, 114, 125, 130, 134, 135),[70] sometimes to Isaiah's Angel of Great Counsel (e.g., *Dial.* 126), and sometimes to an archangel (e.g., *Dial.* 34).[71] He is, further, careful to specify why Christ can be spoken of as an angel. He can be called Angel because "He delivered the messages of God, the Creator of all, to whomsoever God desires" (*Dial.* 56), "in order that by (this) expression you may recognize Him as the minister of the Father" (*Dial.* 58), "because He came to men (since by that power the Father's messages are communicated to men)" (*Dial.* 128). Justin is also careful to specify that although as the *mal'ach* Christ appeared under the guise of incorporeal beings, in the incarnation he has become man (e.g., 1 *Apol.* 63).

The need in the *Dialogue* to argue from Scripture for the Son as distinct from the Father doubtless prompted Justin to make use of the Angel-Wisdom-Word-Son category to an extent not found in his more Gentile-oriented apologies. When he needed to talk to a Hellenistic Jew, Justin employed the Hellenistic-Jewish mythology of a divine redeemer figure—Word—Wisdom—Son—Angel—to speak of Jesus. When he spoke to Gentiles, he used primarily the

Word-Son categories, with the Logos understood in terms of the immanent logos of the Stoics.

The Shepherd of Hermas offers another example of a second-century Christian's appropriation of one variety of the Hellenistic-Jewish mythology. Hermas is primarily concerned about the period after Christ's ascension and before the parousia. Very little is said about activities of the savior before the ascension. Whenever he does refer to such a time (e.g., *Sim.* 5:6:3–8), the pattern is preexistence—incarnation (connected with cleansing the sins of the people)—ascent or exaltation. After his ascent the redemptive activities of the savior continue. In this connection we meet a most reverend or glorious angel who is identified with Christ.[72] This angel justifies those doing penance (*Mand.* 5:7), judges souls, rewards the just, bestows grace, incorporates men into the church (*Sim.* 8:1:1–2; 8:2:1–4), and tests Christians like Hermas (*Sim.* 7:1,2,5). His functions make it difficult to distinguish between God and his angel. This makes it seem that we are nearer to the Old Testament understanding of the *mal'ach* than to any specific figure in later angelology.[73] Yet in *Similitude* 8:3:2–3 a glorious angel is identified with Michael. Here is a notorious crux. Is Christ identified with Michael[74] or is the archangel a separate figure still?[75] Even if Michael is to be distinguished from Christ, as seems necessary, the church's savior is elsewhere identified with the chief of the archangels. For example, Christ is the Son of God in the midst of the six glorious angels (archangels) of which he is chief (*Sim.* 9:12:8; cf. *Sim.* 5:6:4, 7). It would seem, then, that in Hermas the *mal'ach* and the archangel traditions of Judaism have merged, with the archangel dominating. Most instructive is Hermas' identification of the glorious angel with the Son of God and with the Holy Spirit (*Sim.* 9:1:1–3; cf. *Sim.* 5:6:5–7).[76] The redeemer can, in the same context, be spoken of as the "splendid man" (*Sim.* 9:12:8). In Hermas, then, the savior is described basically in terms of an angelology which has coalesced with the categories of Son and Spirit. This is virtually identical with the thought forms of the *Prayer of Joseph*. It is also similar to the position of Justin and doubtless ultimately comes from the same root, Hellenistic Judaism. Nevertheless, the differences between

Justin and Hermas make it probable that each is using a different version of the Jewish mythology.

Sibylline Oracle 8, which probably comes from the period before 180 C.E.,[77] confronts us with the preexistent Word (446). In describing the Word's relation to creation (447–455), though the term *Wisdom* is not used, there are echoes of Proverbs 8:22ff. The incarnation is then described (456–474).

> From heaven he came. . . .
> First . . . the holy, mighty form of Gabriel was displayed.
> And second the archangel addressed the maiden in speech. . . .
> Thus speaking, God breathed grace into the sweet maiden.
> . . . The Word flew into her body,
> Made flesh in time. . . . this, a great wonder to mortals,
> Is no great wonder to God the Father and to God the Son.
> Bethlehem was chosen the homeland . . . of the Logos.[78]

Here we have a synthesis of Angel—Word—Son with possible echoes of Wisdom. If 462 uses God synonymously with archangel, then we also have a blending of archangel- and *mal'ach*-traditions. Significantly, the point at which the angelology is used is at the descent from heaven. Once again, the Jewish roots of the thought and language seem obvious, although the differences between the form here and in Justin and Hermas point to the varieties in which the Jewish mythology circulated.

In Justin, Hermas, and *Sibylline Oracle* 8, the angel component is central in the forms of the myth appropriated by the Christians. Other Christian authors of the second or early third century reflect the same Jewish world of thought but are reluctant to accept it in a form which includes an angel ingredient. Three examples, the *Epistle of the Apostles*, Tertullian, and the *Odes of Solomon*, illustrate the matter.

The *Epistle of the Apostles*[79] knows the Hellenistic Jewish synthesis of Son—Word—Wisdom—Angel but uses it in a significantly different way from that of Justin, Hermas, and *Sibylline Oracle* 8. In Chapter 3 we are told that Jesus *is* the Son sent by God and the Word become flesh. In 13, however, Jesus is not identified with but rather *puts on* the Wisdom of the Father. In 14, Christ *takes the form* of the angel Gabriel and appears to Mary "in the appearance of the shape of an angel." This does not identify Christ and Gabriel.[80] It rather indicates the reluctance of this author to regard Jesus as an angel. Christ rather takes the form of Gabriel in his function as messenger of God, that is, in his descent.

In the works of Tertullian we find an excellent example of the tendency to separate the Wisdom-Logos-Son-Spirit part of the myth from the angel component, doubtlessly because of the context of controversy in which the North African worked. On the one hand, Tertullian employed the familiar cluster, Wisdom—Word—Son—Spirit, to speak of Christ.[81] He also was not adverse to identifying Christ with the *mal'ach* Yahweh who met Abraham under the tree at Mamre.[82] On the other hand, he resisted any attempt to understand the incarnation, as some heretics like Apelles did, by analogy with the flesh of angels when they appear among men. Unlike the corporeality of angels, the flesh of the incarnate Word was that which could suffer and die, that is, the flesh preceded by birth.[83] The heretics, obviously drawing on an existing strand of Christology, argued: Christ bore the nature of an angel. To which Tertullian responded: It is true that Christ has been called "the Angel of Great Counsel," but that expresses his *official function as messenger rather than his nature*. He is not on this account to be regarded as an angel like Gabriel or Michael. Knowing, however, that angel terminology was indigenous to some Christology, "if such an expression is to be hazarded," Tertullian preferred to say, "that the Son is actually an angel, that is, a messenger from the Father, than that there is an angel in the Son."[84]

It is obvious that Tertullian's distaste for angel Christology derives in large measure from its docetic implications. It leads to a denial of the real human nature of the incarnate one. His particular situation may very well be indicative of the larger scene in which angel Christology was gradually eliminated, in part, due to its potential for heretical abuse.[85] In any case, in Tertullian we can see the full-scale synthesis breaking up under the pressure of false belief with the Son-Word-Wisdom-Spirit cluster separating from the angel component.[86]

In the *Odes of Solomon*[87] the break with an angel component is

complete. This early Christian hymnbook speaks of a savior figure
(*Odes* 12, 29, 37, 41, 42), Christ, whose activity in redemption is
described in terms of a *descent-ascent* pattern (*Odes* 12, 22, 23).
The dominant name for the Christian's redeemer is *the Word* (*Odes*
12, 16, 29, 37, 41). At points the divine Word is spoken of in
language that echoes the heavenly Wisdom of Proverbs 8.[88] He
can also be described as the Son of God (e.g., *Odes* 36, 41, 42)
and as the Man or Son of Man (*Odes* 36, 41). In *Ode* 41 we
hear: "His word is with us. . . . The Savior who gives life. . . .
(11) The Man who humbled Himself. . . . (12) The Son of the
Most High appeared. . . . (13) And light dawned from the Word.
. . . (14)" The clustering of the names Word—Son—Man for the
descending-ascending redeemer is significant in two ways. On the
one hand, it argues for the Jewish roots of the mythology here
employed for Christ;[90] on the other hand, it reveals a form of the
myth apparently devoid of an angel ingredient.

It cannot be fortuitous that these Christian authors, when speaking of the church's savior who was preexistent, descended among
men, and then ascended into the heavens, used clusters of titles
such as Word—Wisdom—Son—Angel—Spirit. Such a cluster
existed from pre-Christian times in certain circles of Hellenistic
Judaism and was used for a heavenly redeemer figure. The conclusion must surely be that these writers of the second and third centuries derived their categories from the mythology of Hellenistic
Judaism. At the very least, therefore, one must say that *a* source
for early Christian redeemer mythology is Hellenistic Judaism.

Having seen that certain second- and early third-century Christian authors used the Hellenistic Jewish mythology of a many-
named descending-ascending redeemer in their speech about Jesus,
we now turn to the New Testament, especially Paul, Hebrews, and
the Fourth Gospel, to see whether there exists any demonstrable
link between their Christologies and the Jewish mythologies appropriated by the noncanonical writers. It will be necessary to show
that these New Testament authors employ not only the same *pattern* but also some of the same *terminology* for their savior figures
as found in the Jewish redeemer myths.

In the seven indisputably genuine *Pauline letters* one finds implicit a pattern of preexistence—descent (redemptive activity)—ascent (redemptive activity)—parousia. A combination of all of these movements within one thought unit in the letters is, to my knowledge, not to be found. Moreover, although the ascent is implied in statements about Christ's being at the right hand of God (e.g., Rom. 8:34b; 1 Cor. 15:24–27) or about his future coming (e.g., 1 Thess. 1:10; 4:16–17; Phil. 3:20–21), the actual movement itself is rarely spoken of, unless one wrongly takes all resurrection statements to be such. Only at Romans 1:3–4, where preexistence is not assumed in the pre-Pauline fragment but is implied in the Pauline redaction, and at Philippians 2:9–11, where preexistence is usually assumed to be found in vv. 6–8, is the exaltation or ascent mentioned explicitly. In only two passages, then, is an ascent (more properly, an exaltation) joined with an implicit or explicit descent (becoming man). Furthermore, in both of these texts the descent is not explicitly for a redemptive purpose. The soteriological effects are the result of the exaltation or ascent. In these two passages, therefore, the pattern is closer to the mythology of the immortals than to any other in antiquity.[91]

Rather than focus on the ascent, Paul normally uses a pattern that combines preexistence—descent (redemptive acts). In doing so he frequently uses formulaic material.[92] (1) In Galatians 4:4f. we find reference to the sending of the Son (ἐξαποστέλλειν) followed by a ἵνα clause that explains the saving significance of the "sending" (cf. John 3:17; 1 John 4:9). Here we find preexistence assumed in a formula that speaks of the sending (descent) of the Son into the world for a redemptive purpose. Nothing is said about what happened afterwards to the one who was sent. (2) Romans 8:3 also uses a formula about the "sending" of the Son, using the verb πέμπειν (cf. John where the phrase "the Father who sent [ὁ πέμψας]" occurs twenty-six times in stereotype fashion). Here again preexistence is assumed and the sending is for a redemptive purpose. (3) Romans 8:32's "gave himself up (παρέδωκεν) for us all" (cf. John 3:16—διδόναι) probably belongs with the "sending" formulae which refer to the descent of the preexistent one rather than to the passion formulae which use παραδιδόναι.

Both Kramer and Schweizer[93] argue for the roots of the "send-ing" formulae in Jewish Wisdom speculation. They note that in the passages where preexistence alone is spoken of (1 Cor. 8:6; 10:4; Rom. 10:6f.) the parallels are to wisdom; the "sending" verbs (ἐξαποστέλλειν; πέμπειν) are found in *Wisdom of Solomon* 9:10 in connection with the sending of Sophia; the purpose of the sending in 9:10 is given in a final ἵνα clause; in the same context, *Wisdom of Solomon* 9:17, like Galatians 4:6, speaks of the sending (πέμπειν) of the Holy Spirit; "sending by God" and the title "Son of God" are combined only in the realm of logos and wisdom speculation of Egyptian Judaism (the "gave" formula may find its background there also [cf. *Wisd. Sol.* 9:17a—ἔδωκας σοφίαν]). The argument, though very persuasive, needs modification. Just as the wisdom tradition could speak of a sending of Wisdom by God for a redemptive purpose, so also could the various streams of Jewish angelology. For example, the *mal'ach* is sent by God in Genesis 19:13, Exodus 23:20–21, etc., and the archangel in Tobit 12:19–20. In certain places (e.g., *Prayer of Joseph*), the angel is the firstborn Son of God. It is possible, therefore, that both major streams of Jewish thought which spoke of a descending-ascending savior figure could speak of God's sending a Son for redemptive purposes. When Paul used such language in respect to Christ, its background was apparently the wisdom tradition, doubtlessly merged with others, certainly with the tradition of the Son and quite possibly with that of the angel. In this connection it is interesting to note that Galatians 4:4ff. precedes a remarkable statement in v. 14 where Christ seems, with no hostile overtones, to be spoken of as an angel.[94]

The descent pattern of 2 Corinthians 8:9, Eduard Schweizer thinks, also derives from some form of wisdom speculation in Hellenistic Judaism. For example, Philo can speak of the riches of wisdom (*On the Posterity and Exile of Cain* 151; cf. *Who Is the Heir?* 126ff.; 182ff.; 230ff.). Hence Schweizer's conclusion: re-gardless of whether or not the myth of wisdom literature goes back to an earlier one rooted in gnosticism, Paul knew only the mythol-ogy of wisdom speculation.[95] To which we might add: and quite possibly, Jewish angelology.

This survey of Pauline christological mythology, furthermore, makes it appear unlikely that the second- and early third-century noncanonical Christians' use of the Hellenistic Jewish *katabasis-anabasis* myth was mediated to them through Paul. There are enough differences to force the conclusion that the apostle and the later Christian writers reflect independent appropriations of different variations of the Jewish synthesis.

The Christology of the Epistle to the Hebrews follows a pattern of preexistence—descent (redemptive activity)—ascent (redemptive activity)—parousia. Preexistence is implied in the prologue's statement that Christ is the agent of creation (1:2). He is said to have appeared (9:11, 26) or to have come into the world (10:5). Of his life in the world, it is said that he was made like his brethren (2:17), tempted as we are (4:15), learned obedience through suffering (2:10; 5:8), suffered death (2:9), offered his body as a sacrifice (10:10), destroyed the Devil through his death (2:14–15). He was exalted above the heavens (7:26), entering into heaven (9:24) or the Holy Place (9:12). He took his own blood and secured an eternal redemption (9:12, 24), making a purification for sins (1:3; 2:17; 7:27). He now lives to make intercession (7:25). He will appear a second time (9:28), a coming which is imminent (10:37).

Among the key titles used for this descending-ascending redeemer in Hebrews are certain of those associated with the mythology of Hellenistic Judaism: *Son of God* (1:2; 3:6; 4:14; 5:5, 8; 6:6; 7:3; 11:28, etc.), *High Priest* (2:17; 3:1; 4:14; 5:6, 10; 6:20; 7:17; 9:11; 11:21) and *Word of God* (4:12–13). Further, in 1:3 Hebrews uses ἀπαύγασμα, "reflection," of the Son. Though the term is found only here in the Bible,[96] it is used of sophia in *Wisdom of Solomon* 7:26 and of logos in Philo, *On the Sacrifices of Abel and Cain* 146. Also in 1:3 Hebrews employs χαρακτήρ, "stamp of his nature," for the Son, a term used by Philo of the logos in *On Noah's Work as a Planter* 18. Further, 1:3 speaks of the Son as "upholding the universe by the word of his power," a concept and language found in Philo's discussion of the logos in *On Noah's Work as a Planter* 8, and in *On the Change of Names* 256.[97] Considering pattern and terminology, it is difficult to resist the conclusion that

the Hellenistic Jewish mythology of a descending-ascending redeemer who was many-named has been appropriated by the author
of Hebrews for his speech about Jesus.

At the same time, there is a very definite polemic against angels
in Hebrews. In 1:4–2:16 the author struggles to assert the su-
periority of the Son over angels.[98] It appears, then, that in this
epistle the attempt to separate the angel component from the Son-
Word-High Priest-Wisdom synthesis is sharper than in the second-
and third-century noncanonical writers which have been examined.
It is, therefore, unlikely that these later Christian authors derived
their use of the Jewish mythology from Hebrews. Again, though
both the canonical document and the noncanonical writings have
their roots, at least in part, in the Hellenistic Jewish myth of a
descending-ascending redeemer variously called by such names as
Wisdom—Word—Son—Angel—High Priest—Man, etc., they
seem to be independent adaptations of a common background.
Further, in spite of their use of a similar Jewish mythology, Paul
and the author of Hebrews obviously are drawing on forms of the
myth with different configurations or components. Given the various combinations possible in the mythology, such diversity should
come as no surprise.

In the Fourth Gospel we find again the familiar christological
pattern of preexistence—descent (redemptive activity)—ascent
(redemptive activity)—parousia. Preexistence is found not only in
the prologue (1:1–3, 10) but also in the body of the gospel (e.g.,
1:30; 3:31; 6:51; 8:58; 17:5, 24). The descent is spoken of in a
number of ways. Two formulae found in Paul are also used in
John: "God sent his Son, that" (3:17) and "God gave the Son,
that" (3:16). Distinctively Johannine descriptions include, "I proceeded and came forth from God" (8:42), "I came from God"
(17:8), "I came down from heaven" (6:38), and "I am from
above" (8:23). By virtue of his coming into the world Christ
makes the unseen Father known (1:18), baptizes with the Holy
Spirit (1:33; 20:22), takes away the sin of the world (1:29), gives
eternal life to those who believe (3:16; 17:36; 5:21, 25–26; 6:51;
11:26), and defeats the ruler of this world (12:31). The ascent is
also referred to in various ways. Christ was going to God

(13:3,33,36), was lifted up (double meaning, 12:32), was glorified (double meaning, 12:23; 13:31; 17:5), is going away (16:7). As a result 'of his ascent, the Gentiles can be included (12:20–26,32), the Spirit is given (14:16–17, 25–26; 15:26–27; 16:7–11, 13–15), Christ prepares a place for his disciples (14:3). The traditional parousia concept is clearly found in the appendix (21:22) and in 5:28–29. It may also be seen in the farewell speech (e.g., 14:2–3), though a certain decision is impossible.

A number of lines of evidence point to the Fourth Gospel's roots in the Hellenistic Jewish *katabasis-anabasis* mythology.[99] The names or titles employed for Christ in John are thòse of the Jewish synthesis: for example, Word—Son of God—Son of man. The background for Logos in 1:1–18 is almost certainly the wisdom myth, assimilated with the logos, of Hellenistic Judaism.[100] The clue to the Son of God language in the gospel seems to be the two formulae already discussed in the section on Paul ("God sent the Son, that"; "God gave the Son, that") which have their background in wisdom-logos speculation.[101] The background for the Johannine Son of man sayings constitutes the major problem. The cause of the difficulty is that in John's Son of man sayings we find two circles of thought, a synoptic type Son of man (1:51; 3:14–15; 5:27; 8:28; 12:34) overlapped by a nonsynoptic Son of man (3:13; 6:27, 53, 62; 12:23; 13:31–32) who descends and ascends.[102] The explanation for the distinctiveness of John's Son of man sayings may very well be that the apocalyptic tradition has been assimilated to the "man" of Hellenistic Judaism, that is, to the many-named descending-ascending redeemer.[103] If so, then the use of the *katabasis-anabasis* pattern for the one savior who is variously called Word—Son of God—Son of man is intelligible.

It is, moreover, possible that John reflects an anti-angel tendency. Certain passages have been so interpreted: 1:51;[104] 5:1–9;[105] the Paraclete sayings which employ the expression "Spirit of truth" in 14:16; 15:26; 16:13;[106] and the Johannine version of the empty tomb where belief in the resurrection is divorced from angelic announcement (cf. Mark 16:1–8).[107] If so, then there is in the Fourth Gospel an attempt to separate the Wisdom-Logos-Son-Man synthesis from the angel component. If not, then it is still true that the Evangelist chose not to employ the total synthesis but only a part of it. In this he is a precursor of later Christian developments. Nevertheless, there is not enough similarity between John and most of the second-century Christians we have examined to posit a dependence of the latter on the Fourth Gospel.[108] Rather we must suppose that John and the non-canonical authors represent independent appropriations of the Hellenistic Jewish mythology. There are also enough differences with Hebrews and Paul in terminology and in emphasis to disallow any assertion of interdependence among them. Again, we seem to be dealing with independent appropriations of various forms of the Jewish mythology.

As a result of this survey of selected noncanonical and canonical Christian writers, it seems probable that the linguistic links between the Christian and Jewish mythologies point to the latter as the source of the former. The early Christian myth of a descending-ascending redeemer was taken over from Hellenistic Judaism.[109] It was this myth which was employed by the fourth Evangelist to order the Jesus material in the Gospel of John.

The *Katabasis-Anabasis* Myth and Graeco-Roman Biography

The myth of immortals was used by Christians and non-Christians alike in narratives about their respective hero figures. To my knowledge, however, no extant Graeco-Roman biography uses the myth of a descending-ascending redeemer as the Fourth Gospel does for Jesus. Why is this so?

Arthur Darby Nock furnished the clue when he said: "It was easy enough for an ancient to think of this mortality putting on immortality . . . but the reverse process was not envisaged."[110] For example, in *Corpus Hermeticum* 10:25 we read: "None of the heavenly gods will leave the bounds of heaven and come down on earth." Celsus contended: "O Jews and Christians, no god or son of god either came or will come down (to earth)."[111] If we allow for the modifications required by Justin's Christian stance, he says a similar thing in his *Dialogue with Trypho* 60: "No one with even the slightest intelligence would dare to assert that the Creator and

Father of all things left his super-celestial realms to make himself
visible in a little spot on earth." Such statements express the general
view of antiquity.

Of course, Augustus could be spoken of as Mercury in human
form, but this was an epiphany in a shape assumed for a moment. It
was like the appearance of Athena to Telemachus in the guise of an
old friend.[112] In such terms the men of Lystra interpreted the
activity of Paul and Barnabas in Acts 14. Likewise, this was how
Marcion understood Christ's coming. He was not born but simply
took on the semblance of flesh for a time.[113] To the Graeco-
Roman mind, for a god to take human flesh and to pass through
birth and death seemed undignified.[114] It is not surprising, therefore,
that Graeco-Roman biographies did not use the *katabasis-anabasis*
myth. One could write about the epiphanies of the gods but not as
biography. If one wrote a biography he wrote of a man; it may
have been of a divine man who became an immortal, but it was not
of a god who had become man. Only if a writer had Christian
presuppositions could he write about a man in terms of the
descent–ascent myth—as, for example, in the Fourth Gospel.

If no Graeco-Roman biographies, even if controlled by myth,
employed the *katabasis-anabasis* mythology, what does this fact
imply for our genre discussions? It seems to me that it is the *fact*
that John, like the synoptic gospels and certain Graeco-Roman
biographies, is ordered by myth that is important rather than which
myth is employed. First, it is customary to regard Mark and John
as belonging to the same genre,[115] whatever it is, even though they
are structured in terms of different myths. If the rule applies to
these two gospels, why not to the mythical biographies? Second,
Clement of Alexandria in his *Miscellanies* 6:15 verbalized a Mediterranean conviction.

> If then, according to Plato, *it is only possible to learn the truth
> either from God or from the progeny of God*, with reason we,
> selecting testimonies from the divine oracles, boast of learning the
> truth by the Son of God, prophesied at first and then explained.

Given this mentality, both myths (immortals and descent-ascent)
would function in similar ways. They would serve to underwrite

the divine authority of the subject so described. Finally, it must be remembered that genres are not wooden, static entities. They develop because an author not only uses a set of conventions to communicate but also deviates from the way those conventions have been used.[116] The fourth Evangelist's employment of a descent-ascent myth should be understood in these terms. He follows the convention of telling the life story of his hero in terms of a mythical structure, but exercises his freedom in varying the myth. This argues that his use of myth in ordering his story of Jesus is the important item for consideration in the genre issue rather than his authorial freedom in choosing a different myth.

To conclude: Chapters 2 and 3 have been concerned with Bultmann's first criterion for genre identification. To be classed with the canonical gospels, documents must tell the life of their hero in mythical terms. First, we have shown that certain Graeco-Roman biographies of philosophers and rulers were controlled by myth. Second, we have demonstrated that these biographies employed the same myth to order their material as that used by the synoptic gospels. Finally, we argued that the fourth Evangelist's use of myth to structure his story was the crucial point in determining its relations to the biographies rather than his authorial freedom in employing a different myth from them. At this point, it is time to turn to Bultmann's second criterion: any documents with which the canonical gospels are to be grouped must be cultic in their function. This will be the concern of Chapter 4.

NOTES

1. The view is closely connected with the name of Rudolf Bultmann. Cf. *Das Evangelium des Johannes* (Tr. from the 1964 ed., Philadelphia: Westminster, 1971) pp. 7–9; *R.G.G.*, 3d ed., Vol. 3, p. 847; *Theology of the New Testament* (New York: Scribner's, 1955) Vol. 2, pp. 6, 12–13, 66.

2. Attempts to find a gnostic *anthropos* figure in Philo have failed. Cf. A. J. M. Wedderburn, "Philo's 'Heavenly Man'," *NovT* 15 (1973), 301–26.

3. Frederik Wisse, "The Redeemer Figure in the Paraphrase of Shem," *NovT* 12 (1970), 130–40.

4. George W. MacRae, "The Coptic Gnostic Apocalypse of Adam," *HeyJ* 6 (1965), 27–35; James M. Robinson, "The Coptic Gnostic Library Today," *NTS* 12 (1968), 377.

5. J. A. Gibbons, "A Commentary on the Second Logos of the Great Seth," unpublished Ph.D. Dissertation, Yale University, 1972.

6. One can agree with James M. Robinson, "World in Modern Theology and in New Testament Theology," in *Soli Deo Gloria*, J. McD. Richards, ed. (Richmond: John Knox, 1968), p. 104, that the gnostic redeemer myth is not in origin a perversion of Christology. It does not follow, however, that Christology is thereby an appropriation of the gnostic myth.

7. Walter Schmithals, *The Office of Apostle in the Early Church* (Nashville: Abingdon, 1969), p. 116; A. Grillmeier, *Christ in Christian Tradition* (London: Mowbray, 1965), p. 98. In addition to the groups mentioned in the text, Grillmeier refers to the Nicolaitans, the Archontics, and the Antitactae.

8. Irenaeus, *Against Heresies* 1:25:1–6.

9. *Against Celsus* 7:8–9.

10. Walter Schmithals, *Gnosticism in Corinth* (Nashville: Abingdon, 1971), pp. 138–41, seems to have the better of the argument against U. Wilckens, *Weisheit und Torheit* (Tübingen: J. C. B. Mohr, 1959).

11. Carsten Colpe, *Die religionsgeschichtliche Schule. Darstellung und Kritik ihres Bildes vom gnostischen Erlösermythus* (Göttingen: Vandenhoeck & Ruprecht, 1961); "New Testament and Gnostic Christology," in *Religions in Antiquity*, J. Neusner, ed. (Leiden: Brill, 1968), pp. 227–42; H. M. Schenke, *Der Gott 'Mensch' in der Gnosis* (Göttingen: Vandenhoeck & Ruprecht, 1962). Since J. M. Robinson's negative review of Colpe's book (*JBL* 81 [1962], 287–89), scholarly opinion has seemed to confirm Colpe's and Schenke's conclusions. E. Käsemann's shift is indicative ("The Problem of a New Testament Theology," *NTS* 19 [1973], 238). W. Pannenberg, *Jesus—God and Man* (Philadelphia: Westminster, 1968), p. 151, sums up the situation: "After Carsten Colpe's book . . . it must be considered very questionable whether in the pre-Christian period there had been a complete redeemer myth that was then merely transferred to Jesus."

12. Wayne Meeks, "The Man from Heaven in Johannine Sectarianism," *JBL* 91 (1972), 44, 68; Schuyler Brown, A Review of *Der Vater, der mich gesandt hat* by Juan Peter Miranda, *CBQ* 36 (1974), 421–22.

This objection has usually been answered by saying John was demythologizing the gnostic myth.

13. Wayne Meeks, *The Prophet-King* (Leiden: Brill, 1967), p. 297.

14. Ovid, *Metamorphoses* 8.626–721.

15. Tacitus, *Histories* 4.83–84. For further examples, cf. A. D. Nock, *Conversion* (Oxford: Oxford University Press, 1933), pp. 85–91.

16. Thomas Fawcett, *Hebrew Myth and Christian Gospel* (London: SCM, 1973), p. 158.

17. I regard the issue as a purely historical question. There are no theological-confessional advantages to either position. In this regard, see the relevant comments of Helmut Koester, "The Theological Aspects of Primitive Christian Heresy," in *The Future of Our Religious Past*, J. M. Robinson, ed. (London: SCM, 1971), p. 69.

18. The insights of Wolfhart Pannenberg, *The Idea of God and Human Freedom* (Philadelphia: Westminster, 1973), pp. 1–79, must be taken seriously. In the biblical tradition we are dealing not so much with the demythologizing of myth as with the interpretation of historical events and persons by means of myth.

19. The Qumran Hodayot seem to speak of wisdom as agent of creation (Ps. 1, col. 1, lines 7, 14, 19) and redeemer (Ps. 14, col. 9, line 23). See Svend Holm-Nielsen, *Hodayot: Psalms from Qumran* (Aarhus: Universitetsforlaget, 1960), pp. 17–18, 146.

20. Reginald H. Fuller, *The Foundations of New Testament Christology* (New York: Scribner's, 1965), p. 74, thinks that this is the myth that underlies each successive stage of the development of the wisdom concept in Judaism.

21. Ulrich Wilckens, "σοφία," *TDNT*, Vol. 7, p. 508. On the problem in general, see Roland E. Murphy, "Assumptions and Problems in Old Testament Wisdom Research," *CBQ* 29 (1967), 110–11.

22. W. L. Knox, "The Divine Wisdom," *JTS* 38 (1937), 230–37; J. M. Reese, *Hellenistic Influence on the Book of Wisdom and Its Consequences* (Rome: Biblical Institute Press, 1970), pp. 45–49; H. Conzelmann, "The Mother of Wisdom," in *The Future of Our Religious Past*, pp. 230–43.

23. B. L. Mack, "Wisdom Myth and Mytho-logy," *Int* 24 (1970), 46–60, especially 51–53; B. L. Mack, *Logos und Sophia: Untersuchungen zur Weisheitstheologie im hellenistischen Judentum* (Göttingen: Vandenhoeck & Ruprecht, 1973).

24. Gilbert Murray, *Five Stages of Greek Religion* (Garden City, N.Y.: Doubleday Anchor, 1951). Martin Hengel, *Judaism and Hellen-*

ism, 2 vols. (Philadelphia: Fortress, 1974), Vol. 1, p. 212, speaks of the widespread tendency in Hellenistic times towards the irrational and the mysterious which could only be known by means of supernatural revelations.

25. Walter Schmithals, *The Office of Apostle in the Early Church* (Nashville: Abingdon, 1969), p. 126.

26. Cf. Anitra Kolenkow, "The Coming and Ascent of a Heavenly Healer—Tobit and Mark," working paper for Mark Seminar, Society of Biblical Literature, 1971.

27. For a discussion of the *mal'ach*, cf. G. A. F. Knight, *A Biblical Approach to the Doctrine of the Trinity* (Edinburgh: Oliver & Boyd, 1953) and, by the same author, *From Moses to Paul* (London: Lutterworth, 1949).

28. Gerhard von Rad, *Old Testament Theology* (New York: Harper, 1962), Vol. 1, p. 287.

29. We have here a pre-Israelite tradition which has been taken over and adapted by Israel, making the *numen* the appearance of the *mal'ach* (von Rad, *OT Theology*, Vol. 1, p. 286). Exodus 3:1ab, 2–4a, 5, 7–8 are J material (J. P. Hyatt, *Commentary on Exodus* [London: Oliphants, 1971], pp. 48, 71). Both in J and in the present JE synthesis, the angel is indistinguishable from Yahweh (v. 2 = the angel; vv. 4, 7 = the Lord). Since the two are interchangeable, it seems legitimate to speak of the "coming down" of the *mal'ach* as well as Yahweh.

30. See n. 29.

31. G. A. F. Knight, in *Trinity*, p. 28, thinks it is the *mal'ach*. G. Dix, "The Seven Archangels and the Seven Spirits," *JTS* 28 (1927), 233–85, thinks the angel of the presence is one of the archangels but one superior to the others.

32. On the archangels generally, see H. B. Kuhn, "The Angelology of the Non-canonical Jewish Apocalypses," *JBL* 67 (1948), 211–19.

33. So G. D. Kilpatrick, "The Last Supper," *ExpT* 64 (1952), 5; Joachim Jeremias, "The Last Supper," *ExpT* 64 (1952), 91–92; Christolph Burchard, *Untersuchungen zu Joseph und Aseneth* (Tübingen: J. B. C. Mohr Paul Siebeck, 1965), p. 143, 146, 151. The Greek text with a French translation can be found in M. Philonenko, *Joseph et Aseneth* (Leiden: Brill, 1968).

34. John J. Collins, "Structure and Meaning in the Testament of Job," *SBL Seminar Papers*, 1974, Vol. 1, pp. 49–50; Howard C. Kee, "Satan, Magic, and Salvation in the Testament of Job," *Ibid.*, Vol. 2, p. 55.

35. The angel came (ἐλθών—3:5b[5]) and departed (ἀπελθόντες—5:2). That this language is intended to convey descent-ascent is determined by the document's general thought world (heaven—earth). That this is so is supported by the interchangeable use of "came" (8:2[3]) and "came down" (κατῆλθεν—16:1[3] for another heavenly being, Satan. There is a question whether the angel is simply an anonymous archangel (so H. C. Kee) or whether the apparent identification of the angel with the Lord in 51:1–2 points to his being the mal'ach. Either way, the evidence is relevant for our purposes.

36. John J. Collins, "Structure," p. 41.

37. Bamberger, IDB, Vol. 1, p. 45; also R. H. Charles, Apocrypha and Pseudepigrapha (Oxford: Clarendon, 1913) Vol. 2, pp. 127–29.

38. The Talmud of Jerusalem, Volume One: Berakoth, M. Schwab, trans. (London, 1886; New York: Hermon Press, reprinted 1969), p. 153.

39. Judah Goldin, "Not by Means of an Angel and Not by Means of a Messenger," in Religions in Antiquity, pp. 412–24. At Qumran, 11QMelch. presents Melchizedek as an angelic redemption figure. 3 Macc. 6:18–31 shows angelic deliverance did not necessarily involve worship of angels.

40. Bamberger, IDB, Vol. 1, p. 21.

41. The Testament of Abraham, M. E. Stone, trans. (SBL, 1972), 71.

42. Morton Smith in "The Account of Simon Magus in Acts 8," in Harry Austin Wolfson Jubilee Volume, English Section, 2 vols. (Jerusalem: American Academy for Jewish Research, 1965), Vol. 2, p. 748, thinks first century; J. Z. Smith in "The Prayer of Joseph," in Religions in Antiquity, p. 291, thinks first or second century.

43. With Jonathan Z. Smith, I take the first-person singular of κατέβην ἐπὶ τὴν γῆν καὶ κατεσκήνωσα ἐν ἀνθρώποις καὶ ὅτι ἐκλήθην ὀνόματι Ἰακώβ to refer to the angel Israel and not to Uriel. This fits with line 29, in A. E. Brooke, The Commentary of Origen on St. John's Gospel, 2 vols. (Cambridge: Cambridge University Press, 1896), Vol. 1, p. 97.

44. The Melchizedek Fragment in Sokolov's manuscript of the early first-century 2 Enoch (cf. W. R. Morfill and R. H. Charles, The Book of the Secrets of Enoch [Oxford: Clarendon, 1896], pp. 85–93) has usually been regarded as Christian in origin (so Charles, p. 85; A. Rubinstein, "Observations on the Slavonic Book of Enoch," JJS 13 [1962], 1–22), though it has also had defenders of its early, Jewish character

(e.g., Jonas C. Greenfield, "Prolegomena," to *3 Enoch* by Hugo Odeberg [New York: KTAV, 1973], pp. xx and xlv, n. 21). From my point of view, Rev. 12 argues for a non-Christian origin for the pattern of an infant's being caught up to heaven by God to escape the chaos of the evil powers and at least a first-century date for it, as does the conjunction of names like *high priest—word of God—power* in the Hellenistic Judaism of Philo's time. Of course, that the pattern and its ingredients existed early does not prove the fragment did or that Melchizedek was linked to them this early. In the fragment, the child born by divine conception and after his mother had died, is delivered from the flood by the chief captain, Michael. He comes down, takes the child, and places him in Paradise. Again an archangel descends and ascends in connection with redeeming activity.

45. The *mal'ach* remains separate in such writings as *Sus.* 55, 59; *Bel.* 34.

46. Gregory Dix, "The Seven Archangels and the Seven Spirits," 243.

47. E.g., Philo, *On Dreams* 1.157, where the *mal'ach* who appeared to Jacob in Gen. 28:13 is understood as the archangel; Neofiti Targum on Gen. 32:25–32, where the *mal'ach* is identified as the angel Sariel (cf. G. Vermes, "The Archangel Sariel," in *Christianity, Judaism and Other Greco-Roman Cults, Part Three: Judaism Before 70*, J. Neusner, ed. [Leiden: Brill, 1975], pp. 159–66). This tendency is continued in later Christian circles (cf. A. Bakker, "Christ and Angel? A Study of Early Christian Docetism," *ZNW* 32 [1933], 258).

48. Gregory Dix, "The Heavenly Wisdom and the Divine Logos in Jewish Apocalyptic," *JTS* 26 (1925), 5; G. A. F. Knight, *From Moses to Paul*, p. 100.

49. Cf. Sirach 24:3.

50. See the instructive discussion of H. A. Wolfson, *Philo*, 2nd ed. (Cambridge, Mass.: Harvard University Press, 1948) 1.253–66.

51. For identification of son and angel, cf. also *Prayer of Joseph*; LXX of Isa. 9:5–6; and Dan. 3:25.

52. Philo, *Confusion of Tongues* 146–47 (Loeb Classical Library).

53. E.g., *On Dreams* 1.230, where the logos is *theos*.

54. Wisdom is many-named (*Allegorical Interpretation* 1.14) just as logos is.

55. Ronald Williamson, *Philo and the Epistle to the Hebrews* (Leiden: Brill, 1970), 415–19, 426 (cf. *On the Creation*, 17 and 146); James Drummond, *Philo Judaeus*, 2 vols. (London: Williams & Norgate, 1888), Vol. 2, pp. 226–27, 235.

56. Williamson, *Philo*, p. 418.

57. Reginald H. Fuller, *The Foundations of New Testament Christology*, p. 81.

58. *Wisd. Sol.* 9:4; 10:6; 18:15–16; 11:17 and 9:1–2. This is not to deny that as early as *Wisd. Sol.* an allegorizing of the myth is found.

59. M. J. Shroyer, "Alexandrian Jewish Literalists," *JBL* 55 (1936), 261–84, points out that whereas most treatments of Philo aim at reconstructing a picture of liberal Judaism, Philo can also be used as a source of knowledge of conservative Judaism in Alexandria. For an example of Philo's interpretive reduction of personal beings to abstractions, see *On the Cherubim* 1.138–40; *On Dreams* 1.40–41.

60. Aristobulus (about 170 B.C.E.), like Philo, believed that if men are to understand the real meaning of the Pentateuch they should not be victims of the mythological conceptions as were conservative Jews. Rather they should employ allegorical interpretation of the myth (Eusebius, *P.E.* 8:10:2). In Aristobulus, logos is already identified with wisdom and regarded as a savior figure that imports knowledge of truth (*P.E.* 13:12:13–16). Philo stood almost at the end of a long tradition of allegorization (R. P. C. Hanson, *Allegory and Event* [Richmond: John Knox, 1959], pp. 41–45), one which had its Graeco-Roman equivalent (S. Sowers, *The Hermeneutics of Philo and Hebrews* [Zürich: EVZ Verlag, 1965], pp. 13–18).

61. Richard A. Baer, Jr., *Philo's Use of the Categories Male and Female* (Leiden: Brill, 1970), pp. 4–5.

62. Kleinknecht, "λόγος," *TDNT*, Vol. 4, p. 89.

63. Bousset, "Eine jüdische Gebetssamlung im siebenten Buch der apostolischen Konstitutionem," *Nachrichten von der K. Gellsschaft der Wissenschaften zu Göttingen* (1915), pp. 435–85.

64. Erwin Goodenough, *By Light, Light* (Amsterdam: Philo Press, reprint 1969), pp. 306–57.

65. *Ibid.*, pp. 334–35.

66. A. D. Nock, *Conversion*, p. 92.

67. *Lives of Eminent Philosophers* 7.135.

68. For Isis as many-named, cf. also *Pap. Oxy.* 11. 1380.

69. *Saint Justin Martyr*, T. B. Falls, trans. and ed. (Washington, D.C.: Catholic University of America Press, 1948), p. 244.

70. In contrast to the *Prayer of Joseph* where the angel Israel is the archangel, in Justin the angel Israel is the *mal'ach*.

71. Cf. 1 *Apol.* 6 where Christ seems to be one of the angels (also the note in *Saint Justin Martyr*, p. 39, n.2).

72. Jean Daniélou, *The Theology of Jewish Christianity* (London: Darton, Longman & Todd, 1964), p. 121; Halver Moxnes, "God and His Angel in the Shepherd of Hermas," *Studia Theologica* 28 (1974), 50.

73. Halver Moxnes, *Ibid.*, 55.

74. So Martin Werner, *The Formation of Christian Dogma* (New York: Harper, 1957), p. 134.

75. So Bakker, "Christ an Angel? A Study of Early Christian Docetism," 257–58.

76. This identification is reinforced by the fact that both the Holy Spirit and the Son are preexistent (*Sim.* 5:6:5; 9:12:2) and associated with creation (*Sim.* 5:6:5; 9:12:2). In this connection, cf. *Vision* 1:3:4 where it is Word and Wisdom that are involved in creation. Hermas apparently knew the synthesis Word—Wisdom—Son—Holy Spirit—Angel though he used only Angel—Son—Holy Spirit for the redeemer in his saving activity.

77. Edgar Hennecke, *New Testament Apocrypha* (Philadelphia: Westminster, 1965) Vol. 2, p. 707.

78. *Ibid.*, Vol. 2, p. 740.

79. M. R. James, *The Apocryphal New Testament* (Oxford: Clarendon, 1955), p. 485, locates it in Asia Minor about 160 C.E.

80. A. Grillmeier, *Christ in Christian Tradition*, p. 59.

81. E.g., Tertullian, *Against Hermogenes* 18, in the context of his argument against Hermogenes' claim that matter was eternal. *Against Praxeas* 7, 19, in the context of his pro-trinitarian argument. In both documents it is primarily with reference to creation, a use dictated by the context.

82. E.g., *Against Marcion* 9; *Against Praxeas* 16; *On the Flesh of Christ* 6.

83. E.g., *On the Flesh of Christ* 6; cf. also *Against Marcion* 9.

84. *On the Flesh of Christ* 14. For the six possible relationships between Christ and angelology in early Christianity, of which this is one, cf. Joseph Barbel, *Christos Angelos* (Bonn: Hanstein, 1941, reprinted 1964), p. 286.

85. Jewish angelogy was certainly docetic: e.g., Tobit 12:19; Philo, *Abraham* 22:18; 2 Enoch 56:2; Josephus, *Ant.* 1:11:2 §197; Targum on Genesis 19:3; Pesikta 57a; Justin, *Dial.* 57. J. G. Davies, "The Origins of Docetism," *Studia Patristica* 6 (1962), 13–35, rightly argues that this was one source of early Christian docetism.

86. The pattern could be broken up even further, with *Logos* being

used for the "Son" and *Wisdom* for the "Holy Spirit," as e.g., in Theophilus of Antioch, *To Autolycus* 1:7; Irenaeus, *Demonstration* 9–10.

87. J. H. Charlesworth, *John and Qumran* (London: Geoffrey Chapman, 1972), p. 109, regards the *Odes* as contemporaneous with the Fourth Gospel, i.e., about 100 C.E. For our purposes, such an early date is not necessary.

88. Rendel Harris and A. Mingana, *The Odes and Psalms of Solomon* (Manchester University Press, 1920), Vol. 2, p. 402.

89. J. H. Charlesworth, *The Odes of Solomon* (Oxford: Clarendon, 1973), pp. 127–28, argues that the Son of man is a christological title in the *Odes*. This has been challenged by S. P. Brock in his review in *JBL* 93 (1974), 623–25.

90. This contention finds support on other grounds in the arguments of J. H. Charlesworth, "The Odes of Solomon—Not Gnostic," *CBQ* 31 (1969), 357–69.

91. Cf. the Romulus tradition in Plutarch's *Lives* where the pattern is: (a) came from the gods; (b) life of virtue; (c) taken up to heaven; (d) given a new name or status with benefits resulting for the Romans, his people.

92. For what follows, cf. W. Kramer, *Christ, Lord, Son of God* (Naperville: Allenson, 1966), pp. 112–22, 127–28, 183–85.

93. Eduard Schweizer, "Zur Herkunft der präexistenzvorstellung bei Paulus," in *Neotestamentica* (Zürich: Zwingli Verlag, 1963), pp. 105–09; "Aufnahme und Korrektur Jüdischer Sophiatheologie im Neuen Testament," *Ibid.*, 110–21; *TDNT* Vol. 8, pp. 375–76. A. Van Roon, "The Relationship between Christ and the Wisdom of God According to Paul," *NovT* 16 (1974), 207–39, argues unsuccessfully that wisdom Christology is not found in Paul.

94. R. N. Longenecker, *The Christology of Early Jewish Christianity* (Naperville: Allenson, 1970), p. 31.

95. Eduard Schweizer, "Zur Herkunft der Präexistenzvorstellung bei Paulus," *Neotestamentica*, p. 109.

96. S. G. Sowers, *The Hermeneutics of Philo and Hebrews*, p. 66.

97. R. Williamson, *Philo and the Epistle to the Hebrews*, p. 411, says that Hebrews 1:2ff. describes Jesus in terms at least similar to those of the Alexandrian wisdom-logos theology. Since Williamson's thesis is that Hebrews and Philo have no direct connection, this is significant.

98. R. G. Hamerton-Kelly, *Pre-existence, Wisdom, and the Son of Man* (Cambridge: Cambridge University Press, 1973), p. 244, says that

this emphasis can be explained only by assuming that the author found it necessary to combat an angel Christology. Worship of angels was a problem for early Christianity (e.g., Col. 2:18; *Kerygma Petrou*; *Asc. Isa.* 7:21, etc.).

99. Wayne Meeks, "The Man from Heaven in Johannine Sectarianism," 46, says: "It is now commonly agreed that the Jewish Wisdom myth in some form lies behind . . . the Johannine christology. . . ."

100. Ernst Haenchen, "Probleme des johanneischen Prologs," *ZTK* 60 (1963), 305–34. The parallels with Torah (cf. Kittel, "λόγος," *TDNT*, Vol. 4, pp. 135–36) are derivative. Because the Wisdom tradition identified Wisdom and Law, eventually the characteristics of Wisdom were transferred to Torah. Cf. E. L. Copeland, *Studia Theologica* 27 (1973), 53, 60. T. E. Pollard's attempt to link the prologue with "knowledge" in 1QS 11:11 is farfetched (*Johannine Christology and the Early Church* [Cambridge: Cambridge University Press, 1970], pp. 10–11).

101. Eduard Schweizer, "Zur Herkunft der Präexistenzvorstellung bei Paulus," 108; Kramer, *Christ, Lord, Son of God*, pp. 113, 116.

102. A. J. B. Higgins, *Jesus and the Son of Man* (Philadelphia: Fortress, 1964), pp. 153–57.

103. This also seems to be the position of Carsten Colpe, "New Testament and Gnostic Christology," in *Religions in Antiquity*, pp. 235–36. C. H. Dodd, *The Interpretation of the Fourth Gospel* (Cambridge: Cambridge University Press, 1958), pp. 248–49, takes the same position but maintains that the Heavenly Man of Judaism was a metaphysical abstraction while the Fourth Gospel speaks of a real person. Dodd's problem was that he read for Philo's position rather than for the myth Philo was interpreting.

104. Thomas Fawcett, *Hebrew Myth and Christian Gospel*, p. 159. Rev. 19:10 and 22:8–9 show that the Johannine circle faced the problem of angel worship.

105. Oscar Cullmann, *Early Christian Worship* (Naperville: Allenson, 1953) p. 86. It is a dubious argument because the best text omits the angel of v. 4.

106. G. Johnston, *The Spirit-Paraclete in the Gospel of John* (Cambridge: Cambridge University Press, 1970), p. 122, contends that John safeguarded the primacy of Jesus by his use of language about the Spirit, rejecting the pre-Johannine identification of the angel Michael with the true spirit of God. Johnston is reacting against O. Betz, *Der Paraklet* (Leiden: Brill, 1963), who takes the fact that in heterodox

Judaism (*Test. Jud.* 20:5; 1 QS 3:18–25; cf. Hermas, *Mand.*, 3:4) we find the concept of an angelic spirit of truth who bears witness and accuses to mean that in the Fourth Gospel the Paraclete is Michael (Betz, pp. 64–66). G. Quispel, "Qumran, John and Jewish Christianity," in *John and Qumran*, pp. 137–55, thinks the background for the notion of two Paracletes in the Johannine circle is the Jewish Christian concept of two angels, Christ and the Holy Spirit (e.g., *Asc. Isa.; Elkesai*). If so, Johnston's contention still holds.

107. I owe this insight to Professor Charles H. Giblin, S. J.

108. The closest are the *Odes of Solomon* which R. Schnackenburg, *The Gospel According to St. John* (New York: Herder, 1968) Vol. 1, p. 145, thinks are dependent on John. J. H. Charlesworth, "Qumran, John and the Odes of Solomon," in *John and Qumran*, p. 135, contends the parallels cannot be explained by literary dependence of the Odist on John or *vice versa.* "The most likely explanation for the similarities . . . is that the Odist and John shared the same milieu. . . ." Cf. also Charlesworth and R. A. Culpepper, "The Odes of Solomon and the Gospel of John," *CBQ* 35 (1973), 298–322. Generally neglected are the similarities between Philo and the Odes. Cf., however, J. T. Marshall, "The Odes and Philo," *Exp.* Ser. 8, Vol. 1 (1911), pp. 385–98, 519–36.

109. At present, the evidence seems to point in the direction of a dependence of both Christianity and gnosticism on Judaism. Cf., e.g., G. W. MacRae, "The Jewish Background of the Gnostic Sophia Myth," *Nov T* 12 (1972), 86–100.

110. A. D. Nock, *Conversion*, p. 237.

111. Origen, *Against Celsus* 5:2.

112. A. D. Nock, *Conversion*, p. 237.

113. Tertullian, *Against Marcion* 1:24; 3:8; 4:7.

114. A. D. Nock, *Conversion*, p. 236.

115. Rudolf Schnackenburg, *The Gospel According to St. John*, (New York: Herder & Herder, 1968), Vol. 1., p. 19; W. G. Kümmel, *Introduction to the New Testament* (Nashville: Abingdon, 1966), p. 142; A. J. B. Higgins, *Jesus and the Son of Man*, p. 153; H. Conzelmann, *An Outline of the Theology of the New Testament* (New York: Harper & Row, 1969), p. 323.

116. Alastair Fowler, "The Life and Death of Literary Forms," in *New Directions in Literary History*, Ralph Cohen, ed. (Baltimore: Johns Hopkins University Press, 1974), pp. 77–94, especially pp. 90–92.

4

Cultic Function

The second foundation pillar for Bultmann's contention that the Christian gospels are not biographies is a certain view of the *Sitz im Leben* of both. According to the critical consensus, the Christian gospels are expanded cult legends, presupposing a Christ cult. Their formation is comprehensible only because of the kerygma of this cult. Graeco-Roman biographies, to this consensus, lack any link with cult. This difference in *Sitz im Leben* precludes the possibility that the canonical gospels and the biographies belong to the same genre.[1]

We have contended that this point implies a certain criterion for establishing genre connections. In order to say that the canonical gospels belong to any ancient genre it would be necessary to show that documents within this type were involved in a cultic function like that of the gospels. In this chapter we will concern ourselves with the question of function, raised by Bultmann. The aim of the chapter is twofold. First, there will be an attempt to classify the Graeco-Roman biographies of rulers and philosophers in a new way in terms of their social functions. The similarity between one particular type of biography in such a classification and the canonical gospels will be highlighted. Second, the evidence for cultic connections of these newly classified Lives will be gathered. Again, the similarities with the canonical gospels will be pointed out.

Before any progress can be made toward our two goals in this chapter, it will be necessary to clarify what is meant by "cult." K. L. Schmidt[2] and Rudolf Bultmann[3] used the term in much the same way that it had been employed in the History of Religions School typified by Wilhelm Bousset, in *Kyrios Christos*. Whatever

other connotations *cult* had for Bousset, its central thrust was that
of "a community gathered for worship." The pre-Pauline churches,
he believed, through their veneration of Christ in their rites and
ceremonies maintained a living and present connection with the
exalted Lord.[4] Hence, for Schmidt and Bultmann to claim that the
Christian gospels presupposed a Christ cult was to say that these
writings emerged from a worshiping community.

Recent scholars, e.g. Hans Conzelmann[5] and Ferdinand Hahn,[6]
are hostile to any use of the term *cult* for early Christianity's
worship. The reason seems to be that today the word is identified
with the sacralization of a special defined area (place, time, per-
sonnel). Hostility toward the use of cult for early Christianity is,
therefore, linked to the rejection of a distinction between the realms
of the sacred and the secular. In the sense of a sacred order
separate from the secular, Christianity, it is argued, knows no cult
at all.

While granting that earliest Christianity, like Jesus, did not recognize the division between sacred and secular realms, one must
also concede that these very same Christians did gather for worship.
This worship, moreover, involved certain rites and ceremonies,
however free and charismatic, in connection with which the Christians experienced contact with the living Lord. If *cult* is taken to
mean merely "the worshiping community with its rites and ceremonies," then its use for early Christianity is possible.[7] The issue
at hand is essentially this: do any Graeco-Roman biographies arise
out of, presuppose, or function in the interests of religious/worship-
ing communities? Or are they produced by their authors simply for
a literary public out of a purely literary context and motives? This
chapter, therefore, must concern itself with the question of the *Sitz
im Leben* and function of ancient biography.

Towards the Classification of Ancient Biography

The established categories of classification for biographies in the
Graeco-Roman world are those of F. Leo:[8] (1) the encomium type
in the tradition of Isocrates' *Evander* and Xenophon's *Agesilaus*
(e.g., Tacitus' *Agricola*); (2) the Peripatetic variety which focused
on the revelation of a man's character through his actions so as to

make a moral point and inspire imitation (e.g., Plutarch's *Parallel Lives*); and (3) the Alexandrian or grammatical kind where more attention is paid to chronology than to character, where a rudimentary attempt is made to weigh conflicting evidence, and where there is an absence of concern for imitation of moral examples (e.g., Suetonius, *Lives of the Twelve Caesars*). Since Leo's study at the turn of the century, another type of biography has entered the spotlight of research, namely, the popular or romantic life (e.g., *The Life of Aesop* and *Secundus the Silent Philosopher*).[9] Such writings demand a fourth category of classification.

These four categories are established on the basis of two primary criteria: their formal arrangement, and their degree of historical reliability. Such a system of classification is, of course, *ex post facto*, purely descriptive. Its value lies solely in its utility. Does it shed light on the problems of ancient biography? Systems of classification, however, can obscure as well as enlighten. It is, therefore, often useful to try new ways of organization to see if they can shed any additional light on the same subject matter.[10]

I propose that we attempt to develop an alternative method of classification of ancient biographies on the basis of the criterion of the *function(s)* of the writings in their social-intellectual-spiritual milieu. If we employ this norm, we can make an immediate distinction between didactic Lives that call for emulation of the hero or avoidance of his example and non-didactic Lives that are unconcerned with moral example. Most biographies in antiquity were intended to instruct or to serve as propaganda. Only the Alexandrian or grammatical-type Lives in Leo's classification can be regarded as nondidactic. The encomium, the Peripatetic, and the popular biographies all come under the umbrella of a propagandistic function.

Since the two previous chapters have shown that Lives of rulers and philosophers, as well as the canonical gospels, had links with myth, it seems of value at this point to determine whether such biographies can be classified in any meaningful way according to function. Among the didactic Lives, certain further functional categories exist among biographies of philosophers. We can distinguish five such types.

Type A—Certain Lives function simply to provide the readers a pattern to copy (e.g., Lucian's *Life of Demonax*). At the beginning of his *Demonaktos* (2), Lucian gives his reason for writing.

> It is now fitting to tell of Demonax . . . that young men of good instincts who aspire to philosophy may not have to shape themselves by ancient precedents alone, but may be able to set themselves a pattern from our modern world and to copy that man, the best of all the philosophers whom I know about.[11]

Type B—Other Lives aim to dispel a false image of the teacher and to provide a true model to follow, such as Xenophon's *Memorabilia*, Philodemus' *Life of Epicurus*, Philostratus' *Life of Apollonius of Tyana*, and Porphyry's *Life of Pythagoras*. Xenophon's *Memorabilia* was a pioneer experiment in the area of the biographical genre. It is best understood as a defense of Socrates against the sophist Polycrates who, in 393 B.C.E., attacked Socrates' memory.[12] Xenophon's objective was to preserve the figure of Socrates from distortion, to present him properly so that his deeds and words might serve as a model for other men. Herculaneum Papyrus 1005 is biographical in its subject matter. The mode of treatment, however, differs from that of the other Lives found in the papyri from Herculaneum. Papyrus 1005 is polemical in tone and consists of a defense of the life and practices of Epicurus and his friends against some unknown assailants. Philodemus' purpose is to preserve a true picture of Epicurus against distortions perpetrated by some one or some group.[13] Philostratus' *Life of Apollonius* was also written to protect a sage from misrepresentation. Philostratus was trying to "rehabilitate the reputation of Apollonius, and defend him from the charge of having been a charlatan or wizard addicted to evil magical practices."[14] In particular, he was defending against the work of Moeragenes whose four books, as Origen tells us,[15] attacked Apollonius as a magician. That this is how the life was understood in antiquity is made clear by both Eusebius and Photius. On the one hand, Eusebius implies that if Hierocles' claims on behalf of the philosopher are accepted, then Philostratus' purpose of defending Apollonius against the charge of wizardry is defeated.[16] On the other hand, Photius explicitly says that Philostratus seeks to deny that Apollonius was strictly a wonder worker. If, in fact, he did perform some of the wonders that are commonly attributed to him, they were the results of his philosophy and the purity of his life. Apollonius was actually the enemy of magicians and sorcerers and was certainly no devotee of magic.[17] In this work, the miracle-working Apollonius of tradition has been transformed into the respectable image of a wandering philosopher with Pythagorean leanings. In so doing, Philostratus believed he was depicting the true man and his way of life over against distortions of them. The background of Porphyry's *Life of Pythagoras* offers a means of recognizing its function. By the middle of the fourth century B.C.E. the name Pythagorean already referred to two radically different groups of men, one the scientific circle referred to by Aristotle, the other the ascetic and pious order mocked by Middle Comedy. These two groups were at war with each other over the true nature of Pythagoras. The later neo-Platonists, Iamblichus and Porphyry, presented yet a third image of the philosopher, one that combined parts of the other two into something new and respectable, though still religious in overtones.[18] Porphyry's *Life of Pythagoras*, then, must also be grouped with those biographies of philosophers which sought to present true pictures in contrast to distortions. In these Lives material that had been used to discredit a teacher was oftentimes taken up and neutralized by its inclusion in a new whole.

Type C—Certain Lives intend to discredit a given teacher by exposé (e.g., Lucian's *Passing of Peregrinus* and *Alexander the False Prophet*). These two satirical Lives by Lucian heap ridicule on Peregrinus and Alexander in hopes of destroying any following the two charlatans might have had.[19] Such writings justify Momigliano's contention that biographies were "used by philosophers at large as a weapon against hostile schools."[20] Type C biographies would provoke Type B ones.

Type D—Other Lives of philosophers had as their purpose to indicate where the "living voice" was to be found in the period after the founder (e.g., a third-century B.C.E. *Life of Aristotle* known to us from fragments;[21] various collections of "Successions" of which Diogenes Laertius' *Lives of Eminent Philosophers* is the best preserved). In these biographies the life of the founder of a philosophical school is followed by a list of or a narrative about his successors and selected other disciples which tells where the true tradition of the school is to be found.[22]

Type E—A final group of philosophers' Lives aim at validating and/or providing the hermeneutical key for the teacher's doctrine (e.g., Porphyry's *Life of Plotinus*; the *Life of Aristotle* used by Andronicus to introduce Aristotle's collected works and in neo-Platonic schools in connection with the exegesis of his works;[23] *Secundus the Silent Philosopher*). Porphyry's *Life of Plotinus*, for example, precedes the collection of Plotinus' works made by Porphyry and is regarded as integral with them.[24]

All but one of these five types of biographies of philosophers have parallels among the Lives of rulers. Type A—Biographies whose purpose is to provide a pattern to copy include Isocrates' *Evagoras*, Xenophon's *Agesilaus* (10:2), and many of Plutarch's *Parallel Lives*. Plutarch's main purpose in writing these Lives was clearly a moral one. He wanted to provide for the imitation of noble examples.[25] In his "Cleomenes" (13), he puts it succinctly: "In all these matters Cleomenes was himself a teacher. His own manner of life was simple, plain, and no more pretentious than that of the common man, and it was a pattern (παράδειγμα) of self-restraint for all."[26]

Type B—Biographies of rulers whose aim is to dispel a false image and establish a true one include Isocrates' *Busiris* (5); Nicolaus of Damascus' *Life of Augustus*; Tacitus' *Agricola*; and Pseudo-Callisthenes' *Life of Alexander*. The last of these offers a good example. Alexander appeared in ancient literature either as a tyrant or as a civilizer, as a despot or as a ruler governed by reason.[27] In the popular or romantic biography of Pseudo-Callisthenes, he is idealized as a god-like king over against the supposed misrepresentations of him elsewhere.[28] Hostile material is neutralized by its inclusion in a larger whole with a positive cast. The true picture of Alexander emerges as a model for other rulers to emulate.

Type C—Such Lives would include the treatment of Busiris by Polycrates and those accounts of Alexander which aimed to discredit the ruler by exposé. Among these would be those by Clitarchus who accompanied Alexander's expedition and wrote of it as a brilliant adventure conducted by a tyrant spoiled by fortune, Curtius' *History of Alexander*, and, in part, Arrian's *Anabasis Alexandri*.[29] The fragments preserved in C. A. Robinson, Jr., *The History of Alexander the Great*,[30] contain the type of charges that would be designed to discredit Alexander: he drank too much (so Athenaeus and Philinus); he unjustly killed Callisthenes the philosopher (so Curtius Rufus and Justin); some of his glory is due to manipulated accounts (so Strabo). Against records that reflected such charges, the *Alexander Romance* of Pseudo-Callisthenes would have been produced.

Type D—No biographies of rulers fall into this category. The structure (a=life of the founder+b=list or narrative of successors) seems to have been found in Mediterranean antiquity only in the circles of philosophical schools. Their need for legitimation of teachers in periods after that of the founder apparently created this distinctive form.[31]

Type E—Philo's *Life of Moses* seems to have been a biography of a ruler that aimed to validate and/or provide the hermeneutical key for the legislation that followed. Among Philo's writings there is one group known as *The Exposition of the Law*. This includes *On the Creation of the World*, *On Abraham*, the lost *On Isaac* and *On Jacob*, *On Joseph*, *On the Decalogue*, *The Special Laws*, *On Virtues*, and *On Rewards and Punishments*. E. R. Goodenough has argued that Philo's *Life of Moses* was an integral part of *The Exposition of the Law*. It functioned as an elementary introduction to the ideals of Judaism. The *Life* forecasts the argument of the *Exposition* (*Moses* 2.45–47) and the *Exposition* includes the *Life* in its summary of points covered (*On Virtues* 52; *On Rewards and Punishments* 53). Hence, the *Life of Moses* was written to introduce the Jewish point of view to an interested Gentile. If the treatise succeeded, then the reader could go on to the *Exposition* suggested in the *Life*.[32]

This proposed alternative method of classification of ancient biographies according to their social functions has yielded substantial results. Among the didactic Lives of philosophers we have uncovered five significant functions performed by such writings. Four of the same five functions, moreover, have been linked with biographies of rulers which have a didactic purpose. The five types of biographies classified according to their functions are found over an extensive period of time. All have pre-Christian examples. All have examples from as late as the second, third, and sometimes fourth centuries. In other words, such Lives would have been in circulation before and at the time of Christian origins.

It is important to note at this point the striking similarity between Type B Lives and the canonical gospels. To some extent, all four of our canonical gospels are shaped so as to dispel a false image of the Savior and to provide a true one to follow. In customary New Testament jargon, our gospels belong to the debates over the legitimacy of the various forms of kerygma in early Christianity, that is, to the arguments over which Jesus is the "true" Jesus and which way of life is the "true" Christian way. Like the Type B Lives the canonical gospels often include the alien traditions and try to neutralize or reinterpret them by inclusion in a new whole. Both Type B biographies of rulers and philosophers and the canonical gospels aim to dispel a false image of the teacher and to provide a true one to follow. This similarity in function offers significant support for the contention that the Christian gospels—Matthew, Mark, Luke, and John—belong to the biographical genre. We are now able to address the central question of this chapter: Are the functions of these biographies cultic?

Certain of these functions evident in our classification system for Lives of rulers and philosophers have already implicitly pointed to a community *Sitz im Leben* for the writings. Now, however, we need to ask explicitly whether or not didactic Lives of philosophers and rulers with the various functions previously isolated had any cultic connections.

Cultic Connections for Didactic Biographies?

The question we are asking in the section is: Were any of the didactic biographies of philosophers or rulers produced, either directly or indirectly, by communities whose existence depended upon some divine or hero figure who was the object of the community's reverence, devotion, and worship? Did any such writings present the hero as the embodiment of the value system which he revealed to the community and by which they were sustained? Such a life produced directly by a religious community would correctly be called a cult legend. If a biography was produced by someone other than the religious community but out of a life or materials derived from the worshiping community or cult, then it would be an expanded cult legend. We want to know whether there are didactic Lives of philosophers and rulers which have such connections with religious or semireligious communities.

In the paragraphs that follow, we will use three different means to determine whether any didactic Lives of philosophers and rulers possessed connections with a cult: myth can be shown to be a clue to the cultic *Sitz im Leben* of certain biographies; the link between the life of a teacher or legislator and his collected teachings or laws can be shown to be a similar clue; and, the use of succession lists or narratives can also be shown to be such a clue.

First, *myth* can be shown to be a clue to the cultic *Sitz im Leben* of certain biographies. Before this is possible, however, we must break out of the box of the view of myth characteristic of much modern biblical scholarship. Exegesis today often works with a conception of myth that sees it as an involuntary concep al form typical of a stage in human intellectual history which has now been superseded.[33] This nineteenth-century understanding must be replaced with one derived from modern comparative religion.

From Malinowski[34] and Eliade[35] has come a view of myth that sees it as a narrative telling how, through the deeds of supernatural beings, a reality came into existence, be it the whole universe or some part of it, like an institution. Myth is a statement of primeval reality by which the present life of mankind is determined. It, furthermore, reveals the exemplary models for all human activities here and now. In this view, myth functions primarily to offer legitimation rather than explanation.

This conception of myth has been integrated into classical studies by B. A. van Groningen.[36] In the Mediterranean world, he argues, the ancient was what was valued. The most ancient (i.e., the beginning) was best. The past fixed the rules. So what happened in a remote past, especially at the beginning itself, was decisive for the whole and forever. "If the Greeks ask what the present reality is, what it must be, and how it should be, they look backward to find the answer. This answer depends upon that which they see or take for granted in the past."[37] So the noun ἀρχή means not only "beginning" but also "sovereignty."

Two different conceptions of the past existed: the historical and the mythical past.[38] In the historical realm, events of the past and present were viewed as of the same quality. Events of the past were related as equal phenomena, differing only by their place in the series (cf. Herodotus and Thucydides). In the mythical sphere, the events of the past were regarded as having a different nature than the historical past or the present. They were seen as the basis of historical reality (cf. Hesiod). If the historical past could explain how every human being is procreated by his parents and they by theirs, it took a myth to explain how mankind as a whole came into being. If history could tell how a craftsman learned his technique from his master and he from his, it took a myth to say how such a technique came to exist at all.

Originally these two realms, the historical and the mythical, were kept separate though joined by genealogical connections. The mythical period was believed to have come to an end before the historical began. Yet the mythical stated the situation which was the basis of historical reality. As such, it both explained and gave a direction for the present. Nevertheless, the two were separate and distinct spheres.[39]

At this point, it is necessary to go beyond van Groningen's research to further conclusions. Given the Greek way of thinking, it is inevitable that communities which had come into being in the historical period (e.g., cities and philosophical schools) would need a myth of origins for their historical existence. Such a myth, however, would be different in a significant way. It would have to speak of a historical founder in mythical terms. By the Hellenistic age, these two realms had begun to merge in certain lives of founders, both philosophers and rulers, which functioned as myths of origin for the communities that arose from them.[40] This was a departure from the earlier Greek practice of keeping the myths of

origin separate from history. In these lives, myth was super-
imposed upon history in such a way that a historical event—a
life—was set apart to function as origin for the history of the
community that followed. In order for the historical career of the
founder to be qualitatively different from the rest of history, it had
to be linked to the realm of the divine in a significant way. This
was done by employing specific mythologies to talk about a founder
(e.g., divine man, immortals, *katabasis-anabasis*). By telling
about the life of a philosopher or ruler in terms of these specific
mythologies, his history was transformed into a myth of origins
which explained the existence of the community and gave a direc-
tive for the life of the community in the present. History and myth
merged and the result was history or biography which functioned as
a myth of origins for the community.[41]

Both Malinowski and Eliade recognize that though myth originated and functioned in this way, it could also be taken over and
used by the conscious art of civilization.[42] When this happened
(e.g., Ovid), the myths were emptied of their religious values and
functions and preserved for their epical or fantastic qualities. When
one finds mythology so employed, however, he can infer that it goes
back to such earlier religious roots as those described by Malinowski, Eliade, and van Groningen.

What has this discussion of myth to do with the potential cultic
connections of biographies of philosophers and rulers? We have
seen earlier that certain lives employ myth in speaking about particular rulers and philosophers (e.g., Porphyry, *Life of Pythagoras*;
Laertius, "Empedocles," in *Lives of Eminent Philosophers*;
Philostratus, *Life of Apollonius of Tyana*; Philo, *Life of Moses;*
Pseudo-Callisthenes, *Life of Alexander of Macedon*). Given the
view of myth espoused by the modern history of religions research,
either these writings in their present form, or some earlier forms
now expanded and utilized in these documents, were linked to
communities founded by these hero figures who were the objects of
the communities' devotion. That is, these didactic biographies
which employ myth are either cult legends or expanded cult legends.

We may focus, as a concrete example for this contention, on the specific case of the *Alexander Romance*. In the Hellenistic world ruler worship falls into two distinct categories: worship paid by individual cities to specific rulers who were founders,[43] and the full dynastic cult which involved a centrally organized cult with a hierarchy of priests appointed by the crown.[44] At Alexandria we find both connected with the figure of Alexander the Great. (1) Although the only positive evidence for the cult of Alexander the Founder is a papyrus of 120-121 C.E. referring to a "priest of Alexander the Founder of the city," it is natural to suppose that such a cult would have existed from an early date, possibly even during Alexander's lifetime. This cult doubtless fell into the framework of honors paid to hero founders in general.[45] (2) The dynastic cult was the family cult of the Ptolemies. In it the living ruler was assimilated to that status of the deified Alexander.[46] The cult originated, according to Diodorus of Sicily (*Library of History* 18:28:4), after the body of Alexander was taken to Alexandria, when Ptolemy honored him with sacrifices such as were paid to demigods. Such cultic acts would have necessitated a legend of Alexander told in terms of an immortal.[47] The current *Life of Alexander* by Pseudo-Callisthenes is doubtless an expanded form of the cult legend shaped so as to protect the ruler from attack and to present a true picture of him.

Second, the link between the life of a teacher or legislator and his collected teachings or laws can be shown to be a clue to the cultic *Sitz im Leben* of certain biographies. In antiquity, juxtaposition of a philosopher's life and teaching/works served as an interpretive clue and as a legitimation for his philosophical stance. The juxtaposition could take place in two different ways. In some cases, the biography of the philosopher was a separate unit *alongside* his collected works. Plotinus' *Enneads*, for example, are preceded by Porphyry's *Life of Plotinus*. At the end of the *Life* (26), Porphyry says: "Thus, in sum, I have arranged the fifty-four treatises, constituting Plotinus' entire work, into six sets of nine: to some of the treatises I have further added commentaries. . . . finally, for all the treatises, except that on Beauty . . . I have written summaries. . . ."[48] Then follow the six *Enneads*. Further, we know enough of the practice of the interpretation of Aristotle's works in neo-Platonic schools to be aware of the practice of using a *Life of Aristotle* alongside his collected works.[49]   In other cases, the teaching, given in a systematic fashion, is included *within* the biography of the philosopher.   Diogenes Laertius, for example, used source materials that gave the life of a philosopher (a) together with a succession list or narrative (b).   He also had accounts of the teaching of various philosophers.   He joined the teaching, the life, and the succession list or narrative to produce an a + b + c pattern in certain of the biographies in his *Lives of Eminent Philosophers*.[50] Further, in the *Life of Secundus the Silent Philosopher* the first part dealing with Secundus' life and vow of silence is followed by a second part in which his teaching is set down systematically in response to twenty questions asked by Hadrian.   The juxtaposition of life and teaching/works is here included within the biography instead of being placed alongside of it as a separate unit.

This juxtaposition of life and teaching, in whichever form, served two different functions.   Both functions grow out of a certain mentality characteristic of ancient philosophical circles, namely, the necessity for a union of life and thought in any teacher.   As Seneca put it:

> Cleanthes could not have been the express image of Zeno, if he had merely heard his lectures; he also shared his life, saw into his hidden purposes, and watched him to see whether he lived according to his own rules.   Plato, Aristotle, and the whole throng of sages who were destined to go each his different way, derived more benefit from the character than from the words of Socrates.   It was not the classroom of Epicurus, but living together under the same roof, that made great men of Metrodorus, Hermarchus, and Polyaenus.[51]

The philosopher's word alone, unaccompanied by the act, was regarded as invalid and untrustworthy.[52]   It is out of this conviction that the first function, that of legitimation, arises.   The life of the philosopher functions as a legitimation of his teaching, no example being clearer than that of Secundus.   Hadrian demanded of the philosopher, in spite of Secundus' vow of lifetime silence, answers to twenty questions.   When he would not speak, the emperor commanded that, if he would not speak, he be taken out and killed.

Privately to his soldiers Hadrian said that if Secundus did reply, he should be executed. If, however, he did not reply even under the threat of death, he should be returned to the emperor. When the philosopher was willing to die for his philosophical vow, he was brought back to the ruler who allowed him to write his answers. Furthermore, since he was obviously a true philosopher who would live and die for his beliefs, his teachings were to be enshrined in the royal library. Here the narrative functions to legitimate what teaching is given later. Since, moreover, a philosopher's life and doctrine were one, either could be used to assist in interpreting the other. His life might help understand his works or *vice versa*.[53] This second, interpretive function is doubtless the one involved in the neo-Platonic use of biographies of Plotinus and Aristotle along-side their collected works.

A similar juxtaposition of a ruler's life and legislation is found in Philo. Its background lies in the Hellenistic concept of the ideal king.

> This extremely complex idea was expressed legally by describing the ideal man as νόμος ἔμψυχος, *lex animata*, the incarnate represen-tation of supreme and universal law. In him that Law, itself unformulated, could become vocal, λογικός; that is, the ideal man had the power of taking a Law which was spirit and divine pur-pose, and of applying it to human problems. Through him the Law, or nature, of God could become statutory laws, and true laws for society could never, it was universally believed, be had in any other way.[54]

Philo, in his *Life of Moses*, depicted Moses as a perfect example of Hellenism's ideal king. Having perceived the invisible good, Moses so modeled his own life after it that he became a paradigm for his subjects. Moses is νόμος ἔμψυχος, the incarnate representation of supreme and universal law. Through him, further, the law of na-ture or God could become statutory laws. It is this statutory law derived from the law of nature about which Philo wrote in *The Exposition*. In making the law articulate Moses began with an account of creation, then set the Patriarchs (the great νόμοι ἔμψυχοι) before the reader, then the fundamental principles of the Decalogue, then a code of actual legislation, then an explanation of the place of the ideal virtues in the Law and the divine sanctions of the whole. In doing all this in *The Exposition*, he was making λογικός, vocal or articulate, the νόμος within him. The entire Pentateuch was to Philo the law of God given by Moses.[55]

Philo's *Life of Moses* and *The Exposition* were written as companion pieces. Philo assumed the reader would have read the *Life* before receiving *The Exposition*. The Gentiles who read this *Life* were intended to see in Judaism the realization of all their own dreams. The Jews had the perfect king, the ideal legislator. If the *Life* succeeded in its purpose it would have awakened in the Gentile a desire to learn more of the Jewish traditions, a desire that would have been satisfied in *The Exposition of the Law*.[56] Philo's biography of Moses, therefore, functioned both as a legitimation of the statutory laws in *The Exposition* (they were proper and authoritative because they were derived from one who was a living law) and a clue to the interpretation of the statutory laws.

What has all of this to do with determining the *Sitz im Leben* of ancient biographies? From what has been said about the Lives of both philosophers and rulers whose biographies are juxtaposed to their collected teaching or legislation, it is clear that they were produced or preserved by religious or semireligious communities and functioned on behalf of their communities' religious or value objectives. In this very general sense, then, these biographies are cult documents.

Third, the use of succession lists or narratives can be shown to be a clue to the cultic *Sitz im Leben* of certain ancient biographies. Philosophical schools in antiquity were frequently involved in controversy. On the one side, there was always the question: Which is the true philosophy? Stoics would attack Epicureans; Epicureans would lash out at neo-Pythagoreans. On the other side, within any given school the question could always be raised: Who represents the true tradition from the founder? Groups within any one philosophical school would vie for recognition as the true followers of the master. Within this context of controversy, biographies functioned as weapons.[57] We have seen that Type C biographies of philosophers aimed to destroy a teacher's following by means of exposé. Type B Lives aimed to defend a maligned

teacher and present his true self for all to see as worthy of emulation. The polemics back and forth between schools utilized these
types of biographies. It was similar with struggles within a given
school. Type D Lives of philosophers attempted by their succession lists or narratives to say where the true followers of the founder
were to be located in the present.[58] The living voice is to be
found with individual D because he received the tradition from C
who got it from B who in turn had it passed to him by A who got it
from the founder. This means that wherever one finds a biography
of a philosopher that contains a succession list or narrative, behind
it stands a philosophical school with its debate over the true followers of the founder. Even if a succession list appears in a purely
literary context (e.g., Diogenes Laertius), one is entitled to infer
that here the original school materials arising out of controversy
have been taken over by the conscious art of civilization for its own
purposes. In origin, the list or narrative functioned as an instru-
ment of a school's attempt to delimit its true tradition.

It is important in this connection to remember that a philosophical school in antiquity was often a religious community as, for
example, the Epicurean school.[59] In his *Tusculan Disputations*
(1:21:48), Cicero speaks of the philosophers who do reverence to
Epicurus as a god. Plutarch in his *Reply to Colotes* (1117 B) tells
how Colotes "while hearing a lecture of Epicurus . . . suddenly cast
himself down before him and embraced his knees," an act reflecting
the way statues of gods were supplicated. Indeed in 1117 C, Plutarch makes the act's meaning explicit. Plutarch also cited the
words of Metrodorus to Timarchus: "Let us . . . (exchange) this
earthbound life for the holy mysteries of Epicurus, which are in
very truth the revelation of a god" (1117 B). Plutarch's description of the collective behavior of the Epicureans is that of a cult
(1117). He speaks of their "roars of ecstasy," their "cries of
thanksgiving," their "reverential demonstrations," and "all that
apparatus of adoration" resorted to in their "supplicating and
hymning" Epicurus. Indeed, Plutarch uses the very term *worship*
to describe certain acts in the lecture hall (1117 C). Cicero,
moreover, speaks of an ongoing banquet (a sacred meal) to honor
the founder of the school (*On the Ends of Good and Evil*

2:31:101). This literary evidence about the Epicureans is supported by archeological evidence about the neo-Pythagoreans. An underground basilica discovered at Porta Maggiore in Rome shows that in the early first century C.E. the Pythagoreans were organized as a mystery cult with Pythagoras at its center.[60] Neo-Pythagorean philosophers, furthermore, no less than rulers, could be linked with holy places. Temples and shrines in various parts of Asia Minor were dedicated to Apollonius of Tyana. The emperor Alexander Severus even erected a statue of Apollonius along with those of other gods in his private shrine.[61] What was true for Epicureans and neo-Pythagoreans held true also for neo-Platonism. Neo-Platonism was less a philosophy than a religion.[62] The three different means employed, therefore, have each in its own way pointed to cultic connections for certain Graeco-Roman biographies.

Having been enabled to see the cultic connections of certain didactic biographies of philosophers and rulers in antiquity, it is now necessary to take a fresh look at the Christian gospels to see whether similarities exist between them and these Graeco-Roman Lives.

Consider first the argument from myth. Not only do the Christian gospels and certain Graeco-Roman biographies use some of the same myths, their mutual use of myth of any kind points to similar roots. If myth is basically an account of origins, and if myth is employed in accounts of historical figures because they are in some sense founders, then both gospels and biographies function in the same way. If they use myth, they are either myths of origin for some community or they are developments of such myths of origin. To claim this for the four canonical gospels is nothing particularly new. To recognize that this function is something they share with a group of Graeco-Roman biographies is a departure from the critical consensus.

Consider next the argument from the presence of a succession list or narrative in a founder's life. The existence of "the Acts" as the second part of Luke-Acts makes this line of reasoning important. Luke-Acts contains an extensive succession narrative as part of its story of the founder's life. In this, it belongs together with those Graeco-Roman biographies of philosophers which also included

succession material within the life of the hero. Since they share
this feature, the same type of inference is possible for both. Luke-
Acts and those philosophical biographies with succession lists/
narratives arise out of a common milieu, namely, communities in
which there exists a struggle over where the true tradition is to be
found in the present. Christian and pagan alike attempted to answer the matter by means of a succession principle.[63]

Finally, consider the argument from the juxtaposed life of a hero
and his collected teaching/legislation. There is, of course, nothing
among the gospels analogous to the Graeco-Roman practice of
placing a biography as an introduction to the collected works of a
philosopher or ruler. Jesus did not write or legislate. If we remember, however, that a brief summary of a hero's teaching could
be given *in* the biography itself, collected around certain topics, and
after the narrative of his life, then the First Gospel may offer a
partial parallel. Matthew presents five blocks of Jesus' instruction
(as the second Moses) around five organizing themes, preceded in
each case by the narrative of his career.[64] In any case, the arrangement of Matthew, together with its contents, has led scholars
to posit a school context for it[65] just as the juxtaposition of life and
teaching/legislation in Lives of philosophers and rulers has
prompted the inference of a communal *Sitz im Leben* for them.

What can we conclude? The evidence has shown that certain
didactic biographies of philosophers and rulers have cultic connections. Furthermore, it has become clear that the very same phenomena which led to the inference of cultic connections for pagan
and Jewish biographies are also present in the canonical gospels
and lead to a similar inference for them. Hence, we are enabled to
answer the question with which we began: Could ancient biographies have a cultic *Sitz im Leben*? They could and did. We,
moreover, know this by means of the same type of evidence from
which such an inference can be made about the Christian gospels.

This chapter has exposed significant connections between certain
Graeco-Roman biographies and the canonical gospels in terms of
function. Not only do some biographies possess cultic connections
but also the canonical gospels fit neatly into the functional types of
Lives. All four canonical gospels resemble Type B Lives; Luke-

Acts belongs to Type D biographies; and Matthew has resemblances to one variety of Type E Lives. This conjunction of similarities in mythical structure and cultic functions of various types between the canonical gospels and certain Graeco-Roman biographies makes a strong case for the gospels' belonging to the biographical genre. The third criterion assumed by Bultmann awaits our attention. To it we turn in Chapter 5.

NOTES

1. Rudolf Bultmann, *History of the Synoptic Tradition* (New York: Harper & Row, 1963), pp. 371–74.

2. K. L. Schmidt, "Die Stellung der Evangelien in der allgemeinen Literaturgeschichte," in *Eucharisterion, H. Gunkel Festschrift zum 60. Geburtstag*, H. Schmidt, ed. (Göttingen: Vandenhoeck & Ruprecht, 1923), pp. 50–134.

3. Rudolf Bultmann, *History of the Synoptic Tradition*, pp. 371–74.

4. Wilhelm Bousset, *Kyrios Christos* (Nashville: Abingdon, 1970), pp. 11, 134, 135, 136, 146, 147, 151.

5. Hans Conzelmann, *An Outline of the Theology of the New Testament* (New York: Harper & Row, 1969), p. 46.

6. Ferdinand Hahn, *The Worship of the Early Church* (Philadelphia: Fortress, 1973), pp. 35, 38–39. R. Bultmann, *Theology of the New Testament* (New York: Scribner's, 1951), Vol. 1, p. 121, takes exactly the same position as that taken by Hahn and Conzelmann. Therefore, he could not mean by cult what they mean.

7. Rudolf Bultmann, *Theology of the New Testament*, Vol. 1, pp. 123–24, 133, agrees with this use of cult in early Christianity.

8. F. Leo, *Griechisch-Römische Biographie nach Ihrer Litterarischen Form* (Leipzig: Teubner, 1901).

9. On the *Life of Aesop*, cf. B. E. Perry, ed., *Aesopica: A Series of Texts Relating to Aesop, Vol. I: Greek and Latin Texts* (Urbana: University of Illinois Press, 1952); *Studies in the Text History of the Life and Fables of Aesop* (Haverford, Pa.: American Philological Association, 1936); L. W. Daly, *Aesop Without Morals* (New York: Thomas Yoseloff, 1961). On the *Life of Secundus*, cf. B. E. Perry, *Secundus the Silent Philosopher* (Haverford, Pa.: American Philological Association, 1964).

10. Serious dissatisfaction with Leo's classification exists. Cf. A. Momigliano, *The Development of Greek Biography* (Cambridge, Mass.: Harvard University Press, 1971), pp. 10, 19–20, 45–46.

11. Jonathan Z. Smith, "Good News Is No News: Aretalogy and Gospel," in *Christianity, Judaism and Other Greco-Roman Cults, Part One*, J. Neusner, ed. (Leiden: Brill, 1975), pp. 24–25, overstates the case when he says that "the characteristic of every major religious biography . . . of the Graeco-Roman period is this double defense against the charge of magic. . . ." He is correct, however, in recognizing that biographies are often apologies, as in Type B.

12. Arnaldo Momigliano, *Development of Greek Biography*, pp. 47–54.

13. Walter Scott, ed., *Fragmenta Herculanensia* (Oxford: Clarendon, 1885), p. 68.

14. F. C. Conybeare, Loeb Classical Library, Vol. 1, p. viii. Cf. *Life* 1.2. Philostratus wrote at the urging of Julia Domna, empress of Septimius Severus, who was of Syrian birth and interested in religious revival. Moses Hadas, *Hellenistic Culture* (New York: Columbia University Press, 1959), p. 175.

15. Origen, *Against Celsus* 6.41. Cf. *Life* 1.3: ". . . we must not pay attention . . . to Moeragenes who composed four books about Apollonius."

16. Eusebius, *Treatise Against the Life of Apollonius of Tyana Written by Philostratus Occasioned by the Parallel Drawn by Hierocles between Him and Christ*, 42.

17. Photius, *Bibliotheca* 44.

18. Werner Jaeger, *Aristotle* (Oxford: Clarendon, 1948), pp. 455–56.

19. Helmut Koester, *Trajectories Through Early Christianity* (Philadelphia: Fortress, 1971), p. 216.

20. Arnaldo Momigliano, *Development of Greek Biography*, p. 84.

21. Cf. I. Düring, "Aristotle in the Ancient Biographical Tradition" (Göteborg: *Göteborgs Universitets Årsskrift*, 1957), 464, 465–66, 345–46.

22. E. Bickermann, "La chaine de la tradition Pharisienne," *Revue Biblique* 59 (1952), 49; W. D. Davies, "Reflections on Tradition: The Aboth Revisited," in *History and Interpretation*, W. R. Farmer, *et al* ed. (Cambridge: Cambridge University Press, 1967), p. 141.

23. I. Düring, *Aristotle*, pp. 82, 105, 106, 157, 200. A. Momigliano, *Development of Greek Biography*, pp. 86–87, contends that the *Vita*

Marciana of Aristotle, minus some accretions, is likely to represent the substance of Andronicus' Life written to introduce his edition of Aristotle about 70 B.C.E.

24. Plotinus, *The Enneads*, S. MacKenna, trans., 3d ed. (London: Faber & Faber, 1956).

25. A. J. Gossage, "Plutarch," in *Latin Biography*, T. A. Dorey, ed. (London: Routledge & Kegan Paul, 1967), pp. 48–49.

26. LCL.

27. T. S. Brown, "Callisthenes and Alexander," in *Alexander the Great: the Main Problems*, G. T. Griffith, ed. (New York: Barnes & Noble, 1966), pp. 225–26. Cf. Lionel Pearson, *The Lost Histories of Alexander the Great* (American Philosophical Association, 1960).

28. Cf. E. H. Haight, ed., *The Life of Alexander of Macedon by Pseudo-Callisthenes* (New York: Longmans, Green & Co., 1955) and *The Romance of Alexander the Great by Pseudo-Callisthenes*, A. M. Wolohojian, trans. (New York: Columbia University Press, 1969). B. E. Perry, *The Ancient Romances* (Berkeley: University of California Press, 1967), p. 36, says it is not a romance but a biography.

29. Curtius was a rhetorician who lived during the reign of Claudius. Arrian 7.27 is an example of hostility to the ruler.

30. (Brown University Press, 1953), Vol. 1 (the fragments), Vol. 2 (the translations of the fragments).

31. Charles H. Talbert, *Literary Patterns, Theological Themes, and the Genre of Luke-Acts* (Missoula, Montana: Scholars Press, 1974), pp. 133–34.

32. E. R. Goodenough, "Philo's *Exposition of the Law* and his *de vita Mosis*," *HTR* 26 (1933), 109–25; *By Light, Light* (New Haven: Yale University Press, 1935), p. 181; *An Introduction to Philo Judaeus* (New Haven: Yale University Press, 1940), pp. 37–54. F. H. Colson, *Philo* (LCL, Vol. 7, General Introduction, p. xiv) agrees with Goodenough.

33. Wolfhart Pannenberg, "The Later Dimensions of Myth in Biblical and Christian Tradition," in *The Idea of God and Human Freedom* (Philadelphia: Westminster, 1973), pp. 1–79. Norman Perrin, *The New Testament: An Introduction* (New York: Harcourt Brace Jovanovich, 1974), pp. 21–26, made a start in moving beyond a nineteenth-century view of myth in exegesis.

34. Bruno Malinowski, "Myth in Primitive Psychology," in *Magic, Science and Religion and Other Essays* (Boston: Beacon Press, 1948), pp. 72–124.

35. Mircea Eliade, "Myth," *Encyclopedia Britannica* (Chicago: William Benton, 1973) Vol. 15, pp. 1132–1140; *Myth and Reality* (New York: Harper & Row, 1963).

36. B. A. van Groningen, *In the Grip of the Past* (Leiden: Brill, 1953).

37. *Ibid.*, p. 61; cf. Plato, *Epinomis* 987e.

38. Van Groningen, *Ibid.*, Chap. 8.

39. *Ibid.*

40. John G. Gager, *Kingdom and Community: The Social World of Early Christianity* (Englewood Cliffs: Prentice-Hall, 1975), p. 11, says: "One recurrent feature of new religions is the need to define sacred time. In historical religions, the idea of sacred time normally takes shape around those events which first brought the community into being—symbol systems express the meaning of these events, rituals revive them, institutions derive their authority from them, and the sacred scriptures preserve a record of them for each new generation." Viewed in this way, the philosophical schools are historical religions whose "lives of the founders" function as scriptural accounts of sacred time.

41. Why did Dio Cassius (*Roman History* 45 and 56) tell the story of Augustus in terms of the myth used for Romulus? As Romulus had laid the foundation for a new order, so also Augustus was believed to have done. Since both men's lives were regarded as primal time for the body politic that followed, both had to be spoken of in terms of myth. Suetonius, "Vespasian," *Lives of the Caesars*, likewise speaks of Vespasian as a miracle-working divine man because he is the first of a new line of emperors.

42. Bruno Malinowski, "Myth in Primitive Psychology," pp. 119–20; M. Eliade, "Myth," Vol. 15, p. 1139.

43. Pausanias 10:4:10. Cf. also *TDNT*, Vol. 3, p. 1026.

44. P. M. Fraser, *Ptolemaic Alexandria* (Oxford: Clarendon, 1972) Vol. 1, pp. 213–14.

45. *Ibid.*, Vol. 1, p. 212.

46. *Ibid.*, Vol. 1, pp. 218–26.

47. In Lucian's *Peregrinus* (27), we learn that before the rogue's death he manufactured myths, coveting altars, expecting to be imaged in gold. Myth and cultic act go hand in hand.

48. S. MacKenna's translation.

49. I. Düring, *Aristotle*, p. 112.

50. Charles H. Talbert, *Literary Patterns, Theological Themes, and the Genre of Luke-Acts*, p. 131.

51. Seneca, *Epistle* 6:5–6.

52. Charles H. Talbert, *Literary Patterns*, pp. 90–99.

53. E.g., Diogenes Laertius, *Lives* 3.47; 10:12.

54. Erwin Goodenough, *An Introduction to Philo Judaeus*, p. 34.

55. Erwin Goodenough, *By Light, Light*, p. 189. The background for this view of Philo was worked out in Goodenough's article, "The Political Philosophy of Hellenistic Kingship," *Yale Classical Studies* 1 (1928), 56–101.

56. See n. 32.

57. See n. 20.

58. See n. 22.

59. John G. Gager, *Kingdom and Community*, p. 134.

60. Robert L. Wilken, "Collegia, Philosophical Schools, and Theology," in *The Catacombs and the Colosseum*, S. Benko and J. J. O'Rourke, eds. (Valley Forge: Judson, 1971), p. 279.

61. Moses Hadas, *Hellenistic Culture* (New York: Columbia University Press, 1959), p. 176. Plato received cultus almost immediately after death and soon could be spoken of as Apollo's son. (A. D. Nock, *Conversion* [Oxford University Press, 1933], p. 175), Aristotle was the object of a hero cult at Stageira. (L. R. Farnell, *Greek Hero Cults and Ideas of Immortality* [Oxford: Clarendon Press, 1921], p. 367).

62. E. R. Dodds, *Pagan and Christian in An Age of Anxiety* (Cambridge: Cambridge University Press, 1965), p. 122.

63. This is fully argued in my *Literary Patterns*, Chap. 8.

64. In spite of numerous objections (most recently, J. D. Kingsbury, "Form and Message in Matthew," *Interpretation* 29 [1975], 13–23; *Matthew: Structure, Christology, Kingdom* [Philadelphia: Fortress, 1975], pp. 1–39), Bacon's five-block structure still seems the best alternative for the First Gospel.

65. E.g., Krister Stendahl, *The School of St. Matthew* (Philadelphia: Fortress, 1968).

5

Attitude

The third foundation pillar upon which the critical consensus is erected concerns the literary implications of an eschatological consciousness. According to Overbeck,[1] the spirit of world negation deriving from early Christianity's eschatological perspective demanded unique literary forms for its self-expression. As expansions of the cross-resurrection kerygma, the eschatological proclamation of the primitive church, the canonical gospels could by no means be biographies. The church's eventual acceptance of the forms of the history of profane literature, furthermore, was an index of the loss of its eschatological nature.

We have argued earlier that Bultmann's use of this pillar implies a third criterion for determining genre connections. In order to say that the canonical gospels belong to any ancient genre it would be necessary to show that in this genre the attitude was world-negating just as in the gospels. In this chapter we will focus on the question of attitude, raised by Overbeck and repeated by Bultmann. The aim of the chapter is twofold. First, we will test Overbeck's hypothesis that an eschatological consciousness is so world-negating that it precludes the use of literary forms from the everyday world. Second, we will attempt to demonstrate, from a basic compositional procedure of the canonical gospels, the dominant attitude pervading these Christian writings and to show that it is one they have in common with certain Graeco-Roman biographies.

Eschatological Consciousness and Literary Form

The critical consensus contends that the canonical gospels must belong to a unique literary genre because they are expansions of the

eschatological message of early Christianity, the cross-resurrection
kerygma. Three questions come quickly to mind, however.

In the first place, would a gospel automatically be unique in its
genre because it was an expansion of the Christian kerygma? Consider certain widely recognized facts. We do not possess any Jesus
material that is to any extent untouched by the post-resurrection
faith of the church. Put another way, each individual tradition and
every layer of material is kerygmatic.[2] Further, parallels do exist
for at least some of the individual forms of the Jesus tradition and
for some of the early collections of material.[3] The gospel parables
certainly belong to the parable *Gattung* of antiquity just as the
miracle stories of the gospels fit into the miracle story *Gattung* of
the Mediterranean world.[4] Likewise, collections of sayings, like
Q, are part of the genre *logoi sophou*,[5] as collections of miracle
stories are of so-called aretalogies.[6]

If the Jesus material at *every* level is kerygmatic, then why may
some individual units and certain layers of material properly possess non-Christian literary analogues while the canonical gospels as
wholes may not? The shift from oral tradition to written materials
cannot account for the assumed discontinuity. Some of the
kerygmatic pre-gospel collections were probably written. Evi-
dently the claim that the canonical gospels are developments out of
the cross-resurrection kerygma—as opposed to other *kerygmata*—
must be assumed to account for the discontinuity. This is tantamount to saying that the cross-resurrection kerygma, unlike other
ways of proclaiming Jesus, was world-negating, that is, eschatological. This leads us to the next question.

In the second place, would a gospel produced by Hellenistic
Christians as an expansion of the cross-resurrection kerygma
necessarily reflect a world-negating mood?

Consider the case of Paul and the church at Corinth. Paul and
the Corinthians possessed a common cross-resurrection kerygma (1
Cor. 15:3–5). The Corinthians interpreted it in terms of an overrealized eschatology (1 Cor. 4:8; 15:12, 19).[7] They had, they
believed, already been raised with Christ. This conviction resulted
in denial of the continuing validity of the institutions of this world,
like marriage (1 Cor. 7). If they were already beyond the resurrection, as their speaking with tongues of angels (1 Cor. 13:1)

proved, then they should live like angels, neither giving nor receiving in marriage. If one was unmarried, he should continue so; if he was married, he should separate from his spouse. In Corinth, therefore, we find an eschatological stance that is almost totally world-negating.

Paul, however, understood the same kerygma in terms of an eschatological reservation (1 Cor. 15:6, 13–18, 51–56).[8] His emphasis on the cross (1 Cor. 1:17ff.) and its corollary, the apostles' sufferings (1 Cor. 4:8–13), had the effect of tying the existence of the Christians to this world. It resulted in a world-affirming stance in the sense that Christians live in this world still, even though they know it is passing away. Hence the apostle supported Christian participation in the institutions of this world, though with certain reservations and modifications (1 Cor. 7, e.g.).[9]

In 2 Corinthians 10–13, Paul again uses the passion kerygma as a corrective.[10] This time his emphasis on suffering-weakness rebuts an overemphasis on ecstasy and miracle, both world-denying phenomena. Again the passion of the apostle, grounded in the sufferings of his Lord, ties Christian existence to this world. In Hellenistic Christianity, therefore, the cross-resurrection kerygma need not reflect a world-denying mood but might rather serve a world-affirming one. The passion kerygma might support a stance for Christians which involved living in the world, participating in its institutions and limitations, at the same time that it demanded they not be of the world. This observation raises yet another question.

In the third place, can one possess an eschatological perspective and still employ literary genres from a noneschatological milieu? The case of Paul and his Corinthian opponents again is instructive. There is no doubt about the fact that Paul's perspective was eschatological, both formally and materially (1 Cor. 15; 1 Thess. 4).[11] Yet at times Paul expressed himself in literary forms common to the Graeco-Roman world. Though Philemon has been regarded as the most informal of the apostle's writings, its similarities to Socratic Letter 30 and Pliny, *Letters*, 9:21 are significant enough to render probable the thesis that it belongs to the same subtype of letter as they.[12] Furthermore, if Hans Dieter Betz is correct,[13] Galatians not only belongs in the apologetic letter genre (cf. Plato's Letter 7) but also employs various devices of the art of persuasion, ancient rhetoric. This means that Paul who supposedly developed his theology from the cross-resurrection kerygma possessed an eschatological perspective that did not exclude use of noneschatological genres from pagan antiquity.

We have already seen that Paul's opponents in Corinth were also eschatological in their outlook, even more radically so than the apostle. Corinthian eschatology was world-denying in the extreme. Yet the "spirituals" whose questions are dealt with in 1 Corinthians either used or consented to the use of a letter in communicating with Paul (1 Cor. 7:1, 25; 8:1; 12:1; 16:1,12). Their extreme form of eschatological consciousness did not prohibit their use of a profane genre, the letter. The "ecstatics" whose charges are answered in 2 Corinthians 10–13 were persons who prided themselves on their rhetorical abilities and regarded Paul's speech as of no account (2 Cor. 10:10). They sensed employment of profane techniques of communication as in no way incompatible with their eschatological consciousness.

These data prove that Overbeck's thesis that an eschatological consciousness was so world-negating that it precluded the use of literary forms from the everyday world is untenable. If we are to compare the attitude or mood of the canonical gospels with that of non-Christian writings in Mediterranean antiquity, we must first accurately define that mood.

The Attitude of the Canonical Gospels

The clue to the attitude of our canonical gospels is supplied by their general method of composition. The issue can be clarified by reflection on Koester's article about four types of primitive gospels.[14] The canonical gospels are not equivalent to, and do not really belong in the same category with, the other three types of primitive gospels (sayings gospels, miracle gospels, revelation gospels). Whereas each of the other three types uses only *one* main kind of tradition to convey its insight into the significance of Jesus, the canonical gospels, as Koester recognizes, are *combinations* of various ingredients. Mark, for example, is primarily a combination of miracle tradition and a passion narrative. At the same time, it includes some sayings material (e.g., Chaps. 4 and 7) and a revelation chapter (Chap. 13). The combination is not merely a collection but is controlled by a definite point of view that gives meaning to each component. The other three canonical gospels would fit the same category of combinations of different types of material with varying points of view into new wholes with perspectives different from their parts. From this characteristic of the canonical four, we may derive the attitude of the documents. It is not total rejection of and abstention from that which is different in point of view. Rather it is an attitude of inclusion of that which differs and of reinterpretation of it by means of its participation in a larger whole with another determining principle. The theological dimensions of this attitude and its resultant compositional procedure may better be understood if we look at the four gospels more carefully.

The quest for the compositional principle used by an Evangelist can be pursued in more than one way. It can be described in terms of an author's use of his sources, if they are known, or it can be delineated in terms of the theological use of various materials by the Evangelist. The first method seems most appropriate for our examination of Matthew and John; the second for Luke and Mark. We begin with Luke and Mark.

In an article several years ago,[15] I attempted to show that in the Lukan community certain facets of Jesus' career (e.g., Jesus' words about the secret presence of the kingdom of God in his earthly ministry and the ascension of Jesus) were being interpreted so as to legitimate an overrealized eschatology among Christians of Luke's own day. The major argument, I contended, which Luke used against this overrealized eschatology was the setting up of certain stages that must transpire before the end arrives. Such a scheme of stages was employed by the Evangelist to locate each part of the Jesus tradition in its proper context in salvation history. Luke was written, locating individual Jesus traditions in a controlling context, in order to indicate the legitimate hermeneutical use of the earthly Jesus. In this view, the Third Gospel belonged to a debate over the legitimacy of certain *kerygmata*. Its method of operation was the inclusion of the various parts of the Jesus tradition in a new whole which controlled the way the parts were read.

There were Pauline roots for this Lukan form of argument. In 1 Corinthians Paul was faced with a group of spirituals who interpreted both the words of Jesus and the passion kerygma in the light of their overrealized eschatology. It seems that Paul's opponents knew a tradition of Jesus' words and used it against the apostle.[16] In 1 Corinthians 4:2 they cited a tradition akin to what is found in Luke 12:42f. as the basis for their judgment of Paul. In v. 5 the apostle responded to their overrealized eschatology with another tradition, one similar to Mark 4:22. Then in vv. 8–13 Paul went on the attack, using materials like those found in Matthew 19:28 and Luke 6:24–25. He identified the apostles, including himself, with those covered by the Lukan Beatitudes. His opponents he set under the judgment of the Woes. Here in this context we meet a controversy, essentially eschatological, that was fought by both sides around the interpretation of Jesus' words. Paul's technique was to include the tradition used by his opponents within the larger context of more tradition. He thereby nullified its overrealized eschatological tendencies and interpreted it in the context of an eschatological reservation.

As we have seen, Paul and his opponents also had in common a kerygmatic tradition of Jesus' death and resurrection. His opponents interpreted this tradition in terms of their overrealized eschatology and denied a future resurrection. Obviously it was already past (1 Cor. 4:8)! In response, Paul used an apocalyptic tradition in 1 Corinthians 15:24–28 which set up stages in the unfolding of God's plan for his creation. This use of a scheme of stages in salvation history was the apostle's device for correcting the eccentric eschatology of his opponents.[17] The tendencies we see in Paul in 1 Corinthians 4 and 15 against an overrealized eschatology are closely akin to what we find a generation later in Luke-Acts. In Luke the words of Jesus with a realized eschatology are set in a controlling context so as to prevent their being taken without a future eschatological point of reference. The whole gospel, moreover, is set up so that salvation history is seen unfolding in certain stages, some of which are still future. The Lukan theological perspective and method of operation have roots in an earlier Christian tradition.

The case of Mark—if a widely accepted interpretation of the gospel is accepted[18]—is similar. When the second Evangelist was confronted with a mentality that focused exclusively on the miracle tradition and other signs of Jesus' *dynamis*—in other words with what is regarded as an illegitimate use of the earthly Jesus—he responded with a gospel in which the traditions of Jesus' authority and power were set in a controlling context dominated by Jesus' passion. The miracle tradition was taken up into a larger whole that included sayings material, a revelation chapter (13), and a lengthy passion narrative. Furthermore, both the teaching section of 8:31—10:52 with its three stylized cycles—Jesus' prediction of his passion, the disciples' failure to understand the necessity of suffering, and further instruction for the disciples[19]—and the apocalyptic section with its warnings against false Christs and prophets who use signs and wonders to lead people astray (13:22),[20] function to exalt a view of Christ and his disciples which emphasizes the passion and to warn against the dangers of following miracle workers as such. The new whole includes but controls the way the miracle material is read.

There are also Pauline roots for this Markan form of argument. In 2 Corinthians 10–13 the apostle was faced with a group of Christians who held to a Christology based on a certain understanding of the miracle tradition. Their view of the Christian life was one that emphasized possession of the divine power of the *theios anēr*, manifested in one's eloquent speech and miraculous deeds. Paul's response, though supposedly boasting about equal accomplishments, always seemed to end up accenting his sufferings (11:23–29) and his weakness (11:30ff.; 12:5ff.).[21] This, of course, corresponded to the christological emphasis he made ("he was crucified in weakness," 13:4). This means that Paul, while accepting the legitimacy of the miracle tradition (cf. 1 Cor. 12:12), viewed it within the controlling context of Christ's sufferings and those of his true apostle. This is a similar kind of theological stance and method to that we find taken in the Gospel of Mark where the miracle tradition is incorporated within a whole controlled by the passion. Again, a gospel's theological and methodological roots seem to be in the soil of the Christian community prior to its time.

Before passing on to a consideration of Matthew and John, it would help to review what we have found out about the compositional procedure of Luke and Mark. In the case of these two gospels, we find evidence that the gospels arise out of a desire to prevent a misuse of the Jesus tradition. The misuse of the earthly Jesus that prompted these two gospels was basically achieved by means of an *absolutizing* of some *part* of the tradition. For Mark's opponents it was an absolutizing of the miracle traditions; for the Lukan opposition it was an absolutizing of the present dimension of Jesus' exchatology. The canonical gospels, in these two cases, functioned so as to prevent the absolutizing of the part by balancing and controlling it with another part or parts: in Mark by the passion tradition together with sayings and apocalyptic; in Luke by the emphasis on the unrealized future. The compositional principle followed by these two Evangelists was that of inclusive reinterpretation. A part with a different point of view was included but reinterpreted by its inclusion in a larger whole. Let us now pass on to Matthew and John to see if they employ a similar compositional procedure. In their cases, insofar as possible, we will work from their use of sources.

Assuming the two-source theory,[22] Matthew can be understood as a synthesis of Mark, Q, and oral tradition peculiar to the Evangelist's church. This new whole has three widely recognized characteristics. (1) It looks, in many respects, like a book of community rules with analogies to 1QS and the Didache. As such it offers guidance to some early Christian church.[23] (2) It is unlike manuals of instruction, however, in that its teaching is given in the context of the career of its hero figure. The discourses are set down into a narrative framework of Jesus' life with definite links between the life and the collected teaching.[24] One finds nothing like this in 1QS and the Didache. (3) There are, within Matthew, a number of passages that read like defenses against a false image of the church's savior (e.g., the genealogy, 1:1–17; the baptism, 3:13–17; the story refuting the charge that Jesus' disciples stole his body from the tomb, 28:11–15). This points to an apologetic function for at least part of the narrative.[25] The gospel in its present form and with these traits is unlike the sources from which it was composed. They were taken up and reinterpreted by their inclusion in a whole with a distinctively new perspective.

The same principle of inclusive reinterpretation can be defended for the Fourth Gospel. Robert Kysar's survey of contemporary investigations on the total process of composition which produced John has yielded a negative conclusion. Scholarship has yet to develop an hypothesis that commands universal support.[26] The alternatives are basically two: the gospel arose out of a reinterpretation of a Signs source[27] or the gospel evolved from a single stream of tradition.[28] On either of these two views, the synthetic model of composition posited for the synoptists seems appropriate also for the Fourth Gospel. If one holds to the existence of a Signs source, then the Gospel of John came into being either as a synthesis of miracle and passion traditions as in Mark (if the Semeia source was only a miracle gospel—so Robinson and Nicol)[29] or as a synthesis of a miracle plus passion/Ur-gospel and discourse material (if the Semeia source contained a passion narrative—so Fortna and Teeple).[30] The union of these varying materials with their different perspectives resulted in a reinterpretation of them in a new whole.

If one holds to the theory of an evolutionary process, such as one finds in Barnabas Lindars' work,[31] then the second edition of the gospel (stage four) was a new whole encompassing stage three's version and additional material so that a new danger experienced by the church, Jewish persecution, could be met. The new traditions were joined with the already assembled old ones in a document with a distinctively new thrust.

Scholars are not agreed upon the character and intent of the Johannine synthesis. The resultant whole can be understood in various ways: as a deepening and enriching of the simple theology of the earlier material (e.g., Fortna);[32] as a chastening and correcting of the supposed errors of the earlier material (e.g., Robinson);[33] or as an expansion of the earlier material so as to defend against a new problem (e.g., Lindars).[34] However understood, the synthesis that is our Fourth Gospel incorporated earlier materials with different viewpoints into a new whole which reinterpreted the parts in light of a novel perspective. On a reading of the Johannine compositional procedure following either of the major options in current scholarship, the similarities with Matthew, Mark, and Luke are apparent. All four canonical gospels utilize the same principle of inclusive reinterpretation.

The protest is sure to be lodged: What other procedure could the Evangelists have followed? That the principle of inclusive reinterpretation was not the only one available is seen from the fact that gospels were written which used basically *one* type of material and *excluded* all others. Such gospels following an exclusive principle of composition existed both before and after our canonical gospels were written (e.g., Q and the *Coptic Gospel of Thomas* as sayings gospels: John's Semeia source or an equivalent and the *Infancy Gospel of Thomas* as aretalogies). Following this principle, alien or differing viewpoints were neutralized by their exclusion from the gospel. An analogous situation where the inclusive and exclusive principles of composition clashed was the Marcionite controversy of the second century. Marcion's canon used material of only one perspective (Luke and ten letters of Paul), excluding all the rest. The Old Catholic Church's canon included Marcion's core in a larger whole which conditioned the way Paul and Luke were understood. The compositional procedure of inclusive reinterpretation followed by the canonical Evangelists was only one of the options open to them in their time. From an observation of such a procedure we can infer the mood of the gospels. It was not total rejection of and abstention from that which was different in point of view. It was rather the inclusion of that which was different and the reinterpretation of it by means of its incorporation in a larger whole with another point of view.[35] How does such an attitude compare with that of Graeco-Roman biographies, especially those from types with previously noted similarities to the gospels?

Compositional Procedure and Attitude in Ancient Biographies

In the Graeco-Roman world arguments over the pros and cons of different philosophers and their claims were carried on, not only by abstract argument (as in Plutarch's *Reply to Colotes*) but also by means of composite narratives or biographies of founders' Lives. Similar debates about the careers of key rulers were also conducted in the same two ways: summary argument (e.g., Seneca, *De Beneficiis*, 1.13, 1–3; 7.2, 5–6; 7.3,2—about Alexander the Great) and biography (e.g., Pseudo-Callisthenes, *Life of Alexander of Macedon*).

These biographies of founders' lives which functioned in debates over the true image of the hero were primarily the Type B and Type C Lives of the preceding chapter. In them there was either an attempt to discredit the philosopher or ruler (Type C Lives) or an effort to defend the subject from distortion—both from enemies without and naïve supporters within[36]—and to present a true picture of him for emulation (Type B Lives). The Type B biographies often reflect the same compositional procedure that we have seen already in the canonical gospels. Several examples make this clear.

1. In Porphyry's *Life of Pythagoras* one finds both material of the philosopher's wondrous exploits which came from his followers who saw him as a divine miracle worker (e.g., 23–30), and stories reflecting his rationality and virtue which came from disciples who looked to him as a rational giant (e.g., 39–52). Both are incorporated in a new whole which subordinates them to a perspective that views Pythagoras as a lawgiver and statesman.[37] The compositional procedure is very much like that of the canonical gospels.

2. In Philostratus' *Life of Apollonius of Tyana* one finds miracle traditions (e.g., 3.38, 39; 4.20; 4.45; 6.43) alongside teaching material and narratives showing Apollonius' virtue. At times there are specific rebuttals of the charge of magic (e.g., 5.12; 8.7 [ix]) with an explanation that his powers were due to a divine impulse. There are specific praises of the sage's virtue. For example, as a result of his teaching and behavior, the gods were worshiped with more zeal and people flocked to the temples (4.41). The mighty works are reinterpreted by their inclusion in the new whole which aims to portray Apollonius truly as one like Empedocles and Pythagoras (1.2). Apollonius' miracles are signs not of magic but by-products of his philosophical virtue or saintliness.[38]

3. Pseudo-Callisthenes' *Life of Alexander of Macedon* portrays the hero as the ideal ruler. A series of childhood experiences point to his future greatness as a king by illustrating his wisdom, his strength, his self-control, his role as peacemaker, his reliance on persuasion instead of war, and his respect for his father. Included

in this narrative are, of course, accounts of the various conquests of
his career. Throughout these, however, it is emphasized again and
again how Alexander acted with virtue. Tyre was destroyed only
after the city rejected Alexander's offer of peace. After his victory
over Darius he did nothing arrogant because of his noble wisdom.
Against the Indians he achieved by wisdom what he could not by
force. In other words, Alexander's use of force is set in the context
of his manifestation of virtue. The result is that he emerges not as
a tyrant but as the ideal ruler governed by reason.[39]

4. Diogenes Laertius' account of Epicurus in Book 10 of his
Lives of Eminent Philosophers reflects the same tendency. Laertius includes material used against the philosopher (e.g., Epicurus
was overindulgent, 10.6; he was a man of ill will, 10.7-8) but
shows it to be false in its picture of the philosopher by setting it in a
larger context with another tendency. Here we have what is basically a Type D biography (a—life of founder + b—narrative of successors)[40] in which the *a* component has been assimilated to Type
B Lives. The result is a mixed form, a Life which serves a double
function: both protecting the founder against false charges and
presenting a true image of him on the one side and indicating where
the true tradition of the Epicureans was to be located after the
founder's death on the other.

Although these four examples are from a period later than our
canonical gospels, the procedure of inclusive reinterpretation they
exemplify existed earlier than the time of Christian origins.
Among the prototypes of encomium biographies Isocrates' *Busiris*
reflects this compositional tendency.[41] Isocrates charges that
Polycrates who had produced an earlier account of the legendary
Egyptian king "imputed to him a lawlessness of such enormity that
it is impossible for one to invent wickedness more atrocious" (5).
In the same context Isocrates indicates other writers have also
maligned the ruler. Throughout his encomium Isocrates states,
"You say, but" (e.g., 7, 31, 36-37). That is, Isocrates includes
material hostile to the Egyptian king but neutralizes it by its inclusion in a larger whole with a viewpoint favorable to the ruler.

Herculaneum Papyrus 1005 is a fragmentary part of a Life of
Epicurus by Philodemus which comes from the first century

B.C.E.[42] This biography contains the same type of hostile material that we found in Diogenes Laertius' later *Life of Epicurus* included in a larger whole which defends the founder of the Epicurean school. The compositional procedure which we are describing existed prior to the time of Christian origins and after the period of our gospels. It was deeply rooted in Mediterranean biographical writing.[43]

From this compositional procedure we can infer something of the attitude of these documents. It is not total rejection of and abstention from that which is different. Rather it is an attitude of inclusion of that which is different and of its reinterpretation by means of its incorporation in a new whole with another determining principle. This is precisely the attitude and the resultant compositional procedure we found to be characteristic of the canonical gospels. Type B biographies of philosophers and rulers share a common attitude with the canonical gospels, insofar as this can be determined from their basic compositional procedure.

The results of this chapter are similar to those of the earlier ones. Once again we have found real similarities between the canonical gospels and certain Graeco-Roman biographies. The attitude of the canonical four is not at all a world-negating one which prohibits Christian self-expression in the literary forms of the profane world. Overbeck's and Bultmann's contention has been shown to be erroneous. We have found the attitude of the Christian gospels in the New Testament to be one of inclusive reinterpretation, insofar as it could be inferred from their basic compositional principle. This attitude and its procedural result we have found to be something the four canonical gospels and certain Graeco-Roman biographies have in common. In terms of their attitude, as well as their mythical structure and cultic function, these Christian writings are very much like certain Mediterranean Lives of rulers and philosophers—in particular, Type B biographies. Given this conjunction of similarities deemed decisive by Bultmann for genre decisions, "it is difficult to believe that on first acquaintance the gospels . . . would not have been considered in the Hellenistic world of the first century A.D. to be 'biographies', to indicate what sort of person Jesus was."[44]

NOTES

1. Franz Overbeck, "Über die Anfänge der patristischen Literatur," *Historische Zeitschrift*, n.f., 12 (1882), 417–72.

2. Günther Bornkamm, *Jesus of Nazareth* (New York: Harper, 1960), pp. 21, 25.

3. K. L. Schmidt, "Die Stellung der Evangelien in der allgemeinen Literaturgeschichte," in *Eucharisterion*, H. Schmidt, ed. (Göttingen: Vandenhoeck & Ruprecht, 1923), pp. 50–140. On p. 125, Schmidt concluded that parallels were important for the parts of the gospels but not for the gospels as wholes.

4. Rudolf Bultmann, *History of the Synoptic Tradition* (Oxford: Blackwell, 1963), pp. 179–205 (parable), pp. 218–44 (miracle), shows this well.

5. James M. Robinson, "On the Gattung of Q," in *Trajectories through Early Christianity* (Philadelphia: Fortress, 1971), pp. 71–113.

6. Helmut Koester, "One Jesus and Four Primitive Gospels," in *Trajectories*, pp. 187–93.

7. The interpretation of 1 Corinthians which follows is widespread: e.g., E. Käsemann, U. Wilckens, H. Conzelmann, J. M. Robinson, H. Koester. *Contra* D. J. Doughty, "The Presence and Future of Salvation in Corinth," *ZNW*, 66 (1975), 61–90.

8. Ernst Käsemann, "Primitive Christian Apocalyptic," in *New Testament Questions of Today* (Philadelphia: Fortress, 1969), pp. 125, 133.

9. James E. Crouch, *The Origin and Intention of the Colossian Haustafel* (Göttingen: Vandenhoeck & Ruprecht, 1972), pp. 123–39.

10. One need not be tied to every part of Georgi's thesis to grant this fact. Dieter Georgi, *Die Gegner des Paulus im 2 Korintherbrief* (Neukirchen-Vluyn: Neukirchener Verlag, 1964).

11. Rudolf Bultmann, *Theology of the New Testament* (New York: Scribner's 1951), Vol. 1, *passim*.

12. M. Luther Stirewalt, Jr., "Review of Kim, White, and White," *JBL*, 93 (1974), 480, asks: "Does Socratic Letter 30 (perhaps a genuine letter of Speusippos) throw any light on Philemon?"

13. Hans Dieter Betz, "The Literary Composition and Function of Paul's Letter to the Galatians," *NTS*, 21 (1975), 353–79. Cf. also Hendrikus Boers, "The Form-Critical Study of Paul's Letters: 1 Thessalonians as a Case Study," *NTS*, 22 (1976), 140–58, and Karl P. Donfried, "False Presuppositions in the Study of Romans," *CBQ* (1974), 351–55 (which refers to Stirewalt's claim that Romans belongs to the subgenre of "letter-essay").

14. Helmut Koester, "One Jesus and Four Primitive Gospels," pp. 158–204.

15. Charles H. Talbert, "The Redaction-Critical Quest for Luke the Theologian," in *Jesus and Man's Hope* (Pittsburgh Theological Seminary, 1970), Vol. 1, pp. 171–222.

16. James M. Robinson, "Kerygma and History in the New Testament," in *The Bible and Modern Scholarship*, J. P. Hyatt, ed. (Nashville: Abingdon, 1965), pp. 130–31; D. L. Balch, "Backgrounds of 1 Cor. 7: Sayings of the Lord in Q, Moses as an Ascetical θεῖος 'Ανήρ in 2 Cor. 3," *NTS*, 18 (1972), 351–64. The work of J. P. Brown, "Synoptic Parallels in the Epistles and Form History," *NTS*, 10 (1963), 27–48, must be used with caution but is helpful.

17. Charles H. Talbert, "The Redaction-Critical Quest for Luke the Theologian," pp. 171–96.

18. E.g., Theodore J. Weeden, *Mark: Traditions in Conflict* (Philadelphia: Fortress, 1971); Norman Perrin, *What Is Redaction Criticism?* (Philadelphia: Fortress, 1969), p. 56.

19. Norman Perrin, *What Is Redaction Criticism?*, p. 45, is a recent example.

20. Leander E. Keck, "The Introduction to Mark's Gospel," *NTS*, 12 (1966), 365; Weeden, *Mark: Traditions in Conflict*, pp. 72–100.

21. Cf. E. A. Judge, "Paul's Boasting in Relation to Contemporary Professional Practice," *Australian Biblical Review*, 16 (1968), 37–50, for the context of Paul's actions.

22. D. J. Harrington, "Matthean Studies Since Joachim Rohde," *HeyJ*, 16 (1975), 375–88, lists as a major trend of the past decade general acceptance of the two-source theory but with greater caution.

23. E.g., Norman Petersen, "So-Called Gnostic Type Gospels and the Question of the Genre 'Gospel'," Working Paper for Task Force on Gospel Genre, *SBL*, 1970, pp. 26–27.

24. Cf. Charles H. Talbert and Edgar V. McKnight, "Can the Griesbach Hypothesis Be Falsified?" *JBL*, 91 (1972), 346–47.

25. C. F. D. Moule, *The Birth of the New Testament* (New York: Harper & Row, 1962), p. 91.

26. Robert Kysar, *The Fourth Evangelist and His Gospel* (Minneapolis: Augsburg Publishing House, 1975), p. 79.

27. Robert T. Fortna, *The Gospel of Signs* (Cambridge: Cambridge University Press, 1970); W. Nicol, *The Semeia in the Fourth Gospel* (Leiden: Brill, 1972); H. M. Teeple, *The Literary Origin of the Gospel of John* (Evanston, Ill.: Religion and Ethics Institute, 1974); E. D.

Freed and R. B. Hunt, "Fortna's Signs-Source in John," *JBL*, 94 (1975), 563–79.

28. Raymond E. Brown, *The Gospel According to John, 1–12* (Garden City, N.Y.: Doubleday, 1966); Barnabas Lindars, *The Gospel of John* (London: Oliphants, 1972).

29. James M. Robinson, "The Johannine Trajectory," in *Trajectories Through Early Christianity*, p. 248 and *passim*; W. Nicol, *The Semeia in the Fourth Gospel*.

30. Robert T. Fortna, *The Gospel of Signs*; H. M. Teeple, *The Literary Origin of the Gospel of John*.

31. Barnabas Lindars, *Behind the Fourth Gospel* (London: SPCK, 1971); *The Gospel of John*.

32. Cf. Robert T. Fortna, "From Christology to Soteriology—A Redaction-Critical Study of Salvation in the Fourth Gospel," *Interpretation*, 27 (1973), 32–45.

33. James M. Robinson, "The Johannine Trajectory," pp. 232–68.

34. Barnabas Lindars, *Behind the Fourth Gospel*, pp. 62–78; *Gospel of John*, p. 51.

35. Helmut Koester has commented that a remarkable feature of the canonical gospels is their power to digest gospel literature and traditions of a different type and christological orientation and to make these subservient to their own point of view (*Trajectories Through Early Christianity*, p. 198).

36. Jonathan Z. Smith, "Good News Is No News: Aretalogy and Gospel," in *Christianity, Judaism and Other Greco-Roman Cults: Part One—New Testament*, J. Neusner, ed. (Leiden: Brill, 1975), pp. 24–25.

37. Werner Jaeger, *Aristotle* (Oxford: Clarendon, 1948), pp. 455–56.

38. Moses Hadas, *Hellenistic Culture* (New York: Columbia University Press, 1959), pp. 175–77.

39. E. H. Haight, ed. *The Life of Alexander of Macedon by Pseudo-Callisthenes* (New York: Longmans, Green & Co., 1955).

40. Cf. Charles H. Talbert, *Literary Patterns, Theological Themes, and the Genre of Luke-Acts* (Missoula, Montana: Scholars Press, 1974), Chap. 8.

41. Philip Shuler, "The Synoptic Gospels and the Problem of Genre," Ph.D. Dissertation, McMaster University, 1975, pp. 120ff., places *Busiris* among the laudatory biographies.

42. Walter Scott, ed., *Fragmenta Herculanensia* (Oxford: Clarendon, 1885), p. 68.

43. Josephus' *Life* is an example of the same procedure in an autobiography. He is concerned to defend himself against the misrepresentations of one Justus.

44. G. N. Stanton, *Jesus of Nazareth in New Testament Preaching* (Cambridge: Cambridge University Press, 1974), p. 135. Stanton, however, refuses to draw the logical inference that the gospels are biographies. He remains within the critical consensus although all of his evidence runs in the opposite direction.

Conclusion

The contention of the critical consensus, following Rudolf Bultmann, that the canonical gospels are not biographies was based on three foundation pillars: the gospels are mythical, the Graeco-Roman biographies are not; the gospels are cultic, the Graeco-Roman biographies are not; and while the gospels emerge from a community with a world-negating outlook, the literary biographies are produced by and for a world-affirming people. These pillars, we saw, represent the implicit criteria assumed to be necessary for showing possible connections between the canonical gospels and any ancient literary genre. There must be similarity in mythical structure, cultic function, and an attitude of world negation.

This volume has granted Bultmann his three criteria and has sought to determine whether or not in fact there are the required structural, functional, and attitudinal similarities between the canonical gospels and the Graeco-Roman biographies. In Chapters 2 and 3 the issue of mythical structure was treated. We found that not only were some Graeco-Roman biographies of rulers and philosophers controlled by myth but also that they employed the same myth as that which ordered the synoptics. In Chapter 4 the question of cultic function was taken up. It was pointed out not only that an entirely new classification of ancient biographies could be made on the basis of social function which exposed remarkable similarities with the canonical gospels but also that certain Lives had cultic connections for many of the same reasons claimed for the Christian gospels. In Chapter 5 the matter of attitude was raised. On the one hand, we found that the claim that the canonical gospels had a world-negating attitude was untenable. On the other hand, we saw that the canonical gospels shared with Type B biographies an attitude of inclusive reinterpretation, insofar as this could be inferred from their method of composition. Our study has shown that there exists a conjunction of similarities (mythical structure, cultic function, attitude of inclusive reinterpretation) between the canonical gospels and certain Graeco-Roman biographies. The implication would seem to be that the gospels and the biographies belong to the same literary genre.

If the canonical gospels do belong to the biographical genre in antiquity, can a more precise location of their place among the subtypes of biography be made? On the basis of evidence assembled in the preceding chapters we may make the following summary assessments. (See pp. 94–98 for our typologies.)

1. Mark is a Type B biography of Jesus. It was written to defend against a misunderstanding of the church's savior and to portray a true image of him for the disciples to follow. This gospel was written in terms of the myth of immortals.. This gives the story of Jesus its overall structure and indicates that the gospel functioned as a myth of origins for an early Christian community.

2. Luke-Acts is basically a Type D Life of Jesus. It was written so that (a) the life of the founder was followed by (b) a narrative of his successors and selected other disciples so as to indicate where in the Evangelist's present the true tradition was to be found. At the same time, the *a* component of the Life has been assimilated to Type B biographies so as to prevent misunderstanding of who Jesus really was and to portray an accurate picture of the founder. Luke-Acts is thus a mixed type. It is also composed in terms of the myth of immortals which gives the two-volume work an outer form and which is a clue to its *Sitz Im Leben*. It is a myth of origins for an early church.

3. Matthew is essentially a Type E biography. It was written so as to present the career of Jesus both as a legitimation of his teaching-legislation and as a hermeneutical clue to its meaning. It is also true that Jesus' life is told defensively at a number of points in order to protect the true image of the church's Lord. In this it is akin to Type B Lives. Matthew, like Luke-Acts, is a fusion of two functional types. Matthew is also told in terms of the myth of

immortals. This contributes to its structure and points to its cultic setting.

4. John is a Type B Life of Jesus. It was written to defend against a misunderstanding of the savior and to present a true picture of him. The Fourth Gospel tells Jesus' story in terms of the myth of a descending–ascending redeemer figure. This is a creative adaptation of the biographical genre and is unlike anything else in Graeco-Roman Lives of founders. That is, its outer form has a different shape due to the different myth. The presence of the myth in the story, however, points to John's being a myth of origins for an early Christian community.

The gospels are biographies, albeit ancient ones. This contention no more denies the creative deviations from Mediterranean conventions by the Evangelists than does the claim that Paul's writings are letters rule out his innovative adaptation of that genre. It does mean, however, that when the early Christians told their story of Jesus, on some occasions they followed the conventions of self-expression that clustered together in what we regard as ancient biography.[1]

NOTE

1. To claim that the early Christians used various subtypes of the biographical genre to speak of Jesus in no way detracts from the distinctiveness of their proclamation. The situation is analogous to that one finds in Genesis 1. The author of Genesis employed the *Gattung* "creation story" such as one finds in Babylonian mythology to communicate his message. His message about creation was distinctively Israelite, though the genre he used was one he shared with his non-Israelite milieu.

Indices

Index of Passages

Tacitus, *Histories*
4:83–84 — 55, 81
4:84 — 65

Vergil, *Aeneid*
6:756–776 — 45

Vergil, *Fourth Eclogue*
— 55

Xenophon, *Agesilaus*
— 13, 92
10:2 — 96

Xenophon, *Memorabilia* — 1, 94

Index of Authors

Theology 82 (1979) 300-3